ACCLAIM FOR DAVID FOSTER WALLACE'S

McCain's Promise

"Wallace's longing for the apparently rare virtues of frankness and sincerity in public life makes him admire John McCain, despite the senator's 'scary' right-wing views.... Wallace manages to show just how political spin-doctoring has evolved since 1972, when Timothy Crouse (in *The Boys on the Bus*) and Hunter Thompson (in *Fear and Loathing on the Campaign Trail*) covered the clumsy attempts at it by the Nixon and McGovern campaign staffs. He is bracingly insightful, too, about the equally cynical process whereby representatives of major TV networks and the mainstream press 'select' their news.... Much of *McCain's Promise* really works out the tension between Wallace the postmodernist obsessed with 'packaging and marketing and strategy and media and spin,' and Wallace the moralist seeking evidence of a rooted and authentic self. It is as though Wallace cannot stop expecting McCain to somehow transcend the deceptions and distortions of the spin doctors and the media and remain true to himself: to the McCain who refused to leave prison in Vietnam, and whose moral character has survived an even longer confinement inside the Beltway."
　　　　　　　—Pankaj Mishra, *New York Times Book Review*

"Watching Wallace play his outrage meter is a little like watching John McEnroe complain about a line call. It's not always the accuracy of the claim that keeps you caring, but the hysterics with which it's expressed."　　　—John Freeman, *Boston Globe*

"Dispatched by *Rolling Stone* to cover the doomed 2000 presidential campaign of Arizona Sen. John McCain, Wallace conveys a genuine disillusionment at the sham of the whole arrangement: the endless political posturing, the robotic news coverage. He figures out pretty quickly that the buzz around McCain emanates mostly from the campaign media, who celebrate his 'piss-and-vinegar candor' while failing to note 'the sometimes extremely scary right-wing stuff this candor drives him to say.'...Wallace is actually writing about something more fundamental here, 'a very modern and American type of ambivalence, a sort of interior war between your deep need to believe and your deep belief...that there's nothing left anywhere but sales and salesmen.'"

—Steve Almond, *Los Angeles Times Book Review*

"Compelling.... 'My own résumé happens to have "NOT A POLITICAL JOURNALIST" right there at the very top,' writes Wallace, and it's that lack of expertise and accompanying jadedness that lends the piece an element of genial curiosity—sort of like a very bright tour guide who's still learning the ropes....More interesting than terminology is Wallace's patient and thoughtful meditation on what McCain's military past—specifically, his five-plus years as a prisoner of war—means about his moral fiber."

—Kevin Canfield, *Atlanta Journal-Constitution*

"Wallace's inexperience as a campaign reporter is an advantage here, leading to unvarnished insights into media hierarchies and the use of negative advertising to depress turnout, an anti-democratic practice that benefits extremist candidates with fanatical supporters. 'In reality,' Wallace scolds apathetic citizens, 'there is *no such thing as not voting:* you either vote by voting, or you vote by staying home and tacitly doubling the value of some Diehard's vote.'   —Ariel Gonzalez, *Miami Herald*

McCain's
Promise

ALSO BY DAVID FOSTER WALLACE

THE BROOM OF THE SYSTEM

GIRL WITH CURIOUS HAIR

INFINITE JEST

A SUPPOSEDLY FUN THING I'LL NEVER DO AGAIN

BRIEF INTERVIEWS WITH HIDEOUS MEN

EVERYTHING AND MORE

OBLIVION

CONSIDER THE LOBSTER

McCain's Promise

Aboard the Straight Talk Express
with John McCain and
a Whole Bunch of
Actual Reporters,
Thinking About Hope

David Foster Wallace

Foreword by Jacob Weisberg

BACK BAY BOOKS
LITTLE, BROWN AND COMPANY
NEW YORK BOSTON LONDON

Back Bay Books / Little, Brown and Company
Hachette Book Group USA
237 Park Avenue, New York, NY 10017
Visit our Web site at www.HachetteBookGroupUSA.com

First Back Bay paperback edition, June 2008

Back Bay Books is an imprint of Little, Brown and Company. The Back Bay
Books name and logo are trademarks of Hachette Book Group USA, Inc.

McCain's Promise was originally published in December 2005 under the
title "Up, Simba" in David Foster Wallace's nonfiction collection *Consider
the Lobster,* and was published in a heavily edited form in *Rolling Stone* in
April 2000.

ISBN 0-316-04053-3 / 978-0-316-04053-2
LCCN 2008925452

10 9 8 7 6 5 4 3 2 1

RRD-IN

Printed in the United States of America

Foreword

In August 2007, John McCain came through New York to promote his latest book, *Hard Call: Great Decisions and the Extraordinary People Who Made Them.* McCain's editor, Jonathan Karp, was kind enough to offer me one of the hour-long slots set aside for back-to-back interviews in his office. The new book, written with (all right, by) McCain's literary alter ego, Mark Salter, was evidently meant to serve as a kind of *Profiles in Courage* for the Arizona Republican's presidential campaign. It recounted moments in which wise leaders made brave choices: Lincoln's issuing the Emancipation Proclamation, Branch Rickey's hiring Jackie Robinson to break baseball's color barrier, etc. I sampled a few of these vignettes just before our meeting and found them characteristically well done.

But the book, at that moment, seemed rather beside the point. While Salter was hard at work on *Hard Call,* McCain's presidential campaign had fallen apart. Instead of breaking away from the Republican pack, McCain was loping after it from a considerable distance. At that point, McCain was trailing Rancorous Rudy, Mutable Mitt, and possibly even droopy-eyed Fred Thompson in the polls. McCain had raised a pitiful amount of money and quickly run through it. He'd just fired his longtime campaign manager and laid off three quarters of his feuding and divided staff. *Esquire* reported that he was personally scrutinizing the campaign's daily donut order as a cost center. Unlike his first book, *Faith of My Fathers,* the Salter-abetted autobiography that had launched his 2000 bid, *Hard Call* was looking like a tough sell.

I hadn't seen much of McCain since his famous insurgency in the Republican primaries that year, which I covered for *Slate.* Like most other reporters who spent time trailing his campaign, I retained fond memories—of the candidate's unprecedented candor, his gleeful mischief-making, and the sheer fun of hanging around with him. In the intervening years, however, the spirited maverick had seemed to turn into a weary dray. Preparing his presidential bid, he had mended fences—albeit with evident insincerity—with Christian evangelicals, corporate lobbyists, and anti-tax ideologues who composed his party's power base. Worst of all, McCain was making nice to his 2000 nemesis George W. Bush. With a few exceptions, his idiosyncratic conservatism had turned ordinary.

Yet I held out hope that McCain might have not changed really, and that proximity to defeat might put him in the subversive frame of mind I remembered so fondly. So when we sat down, I prodded the Senator politely, but as obnoxiously as I could. I was just back from a book-writing leave myself, I told him, and hadn't been following the Republican primaries very closely (which was true). But from a distance, his campaign sure as hell looked like a train wreck.

"Jacob," he answered with a sigh, "you don't know the half of it." Where another politician would have been spinning madly to disabuse me of the erroneous assumption that he was somehow not on the verge of victory, McCain launched into his own epic kvetch about how screwed up his campaign was. He hadn't been able to raise the money that his aides said would pour in, he'd been wildly overspending, he'd been too inaccessible, and he wasn't connecting with voters. He sounded like he was criticizing his *opponent*. I don't think Mark Salter, who was sitting in a corner of the room, disagreed with anything McCain said. But he was beginning to look a bit queasy.

I apologized that I'd only had a chance to read a little of his book in preparation for the interview.

"I don't expect you to read every part of it," McCain replied, with a gesture that suggested he might not have gotten all the way through this one himself. And here Salter, who was no longer drawing a salary from the insolvent campaign and derives the bulk of his income from McCain book royalties, began to look more seriously dismayed.

The conversation continued in that vein for a spell. I'd riffled enough pages of *Hard Call* to recognize that McCain was trying to bolster his tenuous credentials as an executive by associating himself with heroic figures like Churchill, Reagan, and Truman. Some of the leaders he considered in the book cast a spell through charisma, others through domineering energy, still others through a broad vision of change. But McCain himself didn't seem like any of those leaders, I pointed out. He wasn't charismatic, had little vision of the future, and was more satirist than autocrat. No argument from the author here either. "Whether I'm a leader in the category of people I was just talking about I think is doubtful," he said.

At this point, I glanced over at Salter, whose face was now buried in his hands.

Off, off message, McCain merrily went. What, I asked, did he think about his new best friend George W. Bush as a leader? Why wasn't he in the book? "I think that the very significant failing was to not question the course of the war in Iraq for too long," he said. "I'm told that the president would say to the generals on the teleconference, 'Do you have everything you need?' 'Yes sir!' End of conversation! I think General Eisenhower would have said, well, what about the casualties in Anbar Province? What about the suicide bombers? He'd go down the list of challenges we were facing. How's it going with the de-Ba'athification? What's happening with the oil revenues?"

I noted Bush's curious quality of taking strenuous opposition as proof that he must be right. McCain concurred. "I really feel that to somehow be encouraged by opposition is not a productive exercise," McCain replied. "Because if you continue to have American public opinion opposed to our involvement in Iraq—no matter what I think the consequences of failure are—we're not going to be able to sustain it, period." When I got back to my office, there was a message from Salter saying he hoped I hadn't misconstrued any of those comments as, ahem, critical of the president.

As McCain and I chatted, I found myself transported back to January 2000 on the Straight Talk Express. This was the name given the campaign bus on which the candidate rode around New Hampshire and South Carolina, holding court in the conversation pit with a claque of reporters. More broadly, the Straight Talk Express was McCain's whole caffeinated road show, which lurched intermodally from town hall to fund-raiser to debate, nearly upsetting the front-runner George W. Bush, and threatening to overturn the entire Republican establishment.

To most of those who were aboard at any point, the Express remained a high-water mark in covering presidential politics. Part of it was of course the free-flowing access, which, if you'd chased after Bush, Gore, or most any other candidate, felt like nickel beer after Prohibition. Campaigns ration a candidate's unscripted availability in an effort to stay on message, control his image, and avoid gaffes. But the McCain team took the opposite approach, allowing the candidate to gab so carelessly that his slips ceased to be newsworthy. In the beige leather lounge area, the daily dialogue tended to begin with badinage, delve into political tactics, then dabble in policy, before collapsing into something resembling a conversation among humans about whatever anyone felt like talking about. When the bus stopped, McCain got out and did the same thing with voters at his town hall meetings, indulging in free-associative humor and answering questions about everything with spontaneity and sympathy.

McCain's openness, his incredible life story, and his renegade persona bred a camaraderie and admiration that threatened to break out into the open. The shorthand for the affection the press developed for the candidate was The Swoon. McCain's combination of principled belief and subversive nature made him into an unexpected creature: the Republican dissident. A conservative patriot, he had no respect at all for authority, especially that of his party's moneyed establishment.

His struggle with conscience was fascinating to watch. McCain would behave like an ordinary politician and then flagellate himself mercilessly for having done so. The moment that encapsulates that best for me was McCain's apology for an especially egregious act of pandering, when he said that he saw the Confederate flag flying over the South Carolina statehouse as a symbol of "heritage" rather than racism. After he'd lost the race, McCain went back to Columbia to address his failure. "I feared that if I answered honestly, I could not win the South Carolina primary. So I chose to compromise my principles," he said. Politicians rarely acknowledge as much on their way to prison.

It was in the midst of The Great Swoon, somewhere near Charleston, that I one day noticed David Foster Wallace standing alongside the campaign caravan, trying to talk his way aboard. I was aware that he was coming out on the trail, because his editor, who I knew a bit, had called to see if I could help get him a spot on the lead bus. For *Rolling Stone,* having *writers* cover the presidential campaign was a long tradition. But this assignment struck me as especially inspired. Scraggled, hypertexting author, meet incongruous American patriot. Something interesting was sure to come out of this, at least if the one ever got near the other.

I was no help at all. The most brilliant writer of my generation (I thought then, I think now) was dropping in for a visit, and the McCain people didn't have the slightest clue who he was. That the author wore a ponytail, shaved inconclusively, and was writing for a post–Super Tuesday deadline for a publication regarded as noninfluential on the GOP primary circuit didn't help much either. In such matters, the McCain campaign could be pretty conventional.

The visitor from *Rolling Stone* turned the absence of access to the most accessible campaign in history into an asset, focusing first on the media mechanics. After you've covered road show politics for a while, its rituals begin to seem rational. It takes fresh eyes to observe the essential absurdity and the sheer redundancy of it all: the candidate who goes from place to place repeating the same jokes, the pack of reporters who witness precisely the same speech ("The 22.5"), the labor and expense of hauling gear and technicians in secure conditions, and the fact that 99.9 percent of what happens is never reported at all. It's an environment of privileged deprivation, and that breeds its own hierarchy and groupthink. As an editor, I always give the same advice to young journalists who join this traveling circus: Don't forget to tell us how weird it is.

Wallace doesn't miss much campaign trail weirdness circa the early digital era. This piece is, among other things, a self-conscious ethnographer's take on an alien culture. Wallace describes the circular waltz of reporters talking into their cell phones outside an event as an anthropologist might the rituals of a Hopi Kiva. He does not, however, refrain from a degree of judgment when it comes to the Twelve Monkeys, the top-drawer writing press, who "tend to be so totally identical in dress and demeanor as to be almost surreal—twelve immaculate and wrinkle-free navy-blue blazers, half-Windsored ties, pleated chinos, oxfordcloth shirts that even when the jackets come off stay 100 percent buttoned at the collar and sleeves...plus a uniform self-seriousness that reminds you of every overachieving dweeb you ever wanted to kick the ass of in school." Blocked from the lead bus, he takes up with the sound- and cameramen who rack up overtime babysitting the heavy artillery on the trailing vehicle, Bullshit #1. If you're wondering what the phrase "Up, Simba" (the title under which Wallace's account was previously published) has to do with John McCain, it's the meaningless exhortation of a network tech hefting a $40,000 camera rig to his shoulder to record what the candidate says when the media form a "scrum" around him.

I remain unpersuaded by the author's noble savage conceit that the roadies embody a deeper wisdom about what's happening in the campaign. But Wallace himself did come away from his week on the road with a more sophisticated understanding of the McCain phenomenon than many who lived in his bubble indefinitely. Most important, he grasped a question at the core of McCain's idiosyncratic antipolitics, one that eluded techs and monkeys alike. The root issue, as Wallace sees it, is how to square McCain's evident honor and honesty with the image of a politician angling for advantage.

Wallace approaches this problem by retelling the most famous part of McCain's biography, what happened when the young naval aviator was shot down over Hanoi in 1967. After nearly being lynched by an angry mob, McCain declined an offer of early release, choosing instead to spend the next five years being isolated and tortured in the Hanoi Hilton. Wallace imagines what might have gone through McCain's head when the prison commandant had guards break his ribs, rebreak his arm, and knock out his teeth because he wouldn't accept an early release that accorded with Vietnamese propaganda purposes. Wallace says that none of us can know for sure how we would have reacted in this situation.

> But, see, we *do* know how this man reacted. That he chose to spend four more years there, mostly in a dark box, alone, tapping messages on the walls to the others, rather than violate a Code. Maybe he was nuts. But the point is that with McCain it feels like we *know*, for a proven fact, that he is capable of devotion to something other, more, than his own self-interest. So that when he says the line in speeches now you can feel like maybe it's not just more candidate bullshit, that with this guy it's maybe the truth. Or maybe both the truth *and* bullshit—the man does want your vote, after all.

Here he grasps, I think, the essential McCain conundrum. People respond to John McCain because of his palpable sense of honor, his aversion to pandering, and his patriotic idealism. But at the same time, McCain takes advantage of these qualities to give himself a pass when he behaves politically—running attack ads against his opponent, raising money from interest groups, and sucking up to his party's powerful constituencies. Because we know he's different from the rest, it's not supposed to count when he behaves in essentially the same way others do. "There are many elements of the McCain2000 campaign," Wallace writes,

> ...that indicate that some very shrewd, clever marketers are trying to market this candidate's rejection of shrewd, clever marketing.... Is it hypocritical that one of McCain's ads' lines in South Carolina is "Telling the truth even when it hurts him politically," which of course since it's an ad means that McCain is trying to get political benefit out of his indifference to political benefit? What's the difference between hypocrisy and paradox?

An illustration that comes to mind is a trip I took with McCain in the fall of 1999 to the Reagan Library in Simi Valley, California. Another reporter and I gabbed with McCain across the whole length of the country—on a private jet lent by Rupert

Murdoch. A senator borrowing the plane of a mogul with business before his committee was precisely the sort of cozy corruption McCain inveighed against. But before we could raise the issue, McCain had given us a twinkle and a nudge that said, if not in so many words: *how awesome that we're ripping off that sleazebag Rupert Murdoch!* To live outside the law, as Dylan once said, you must be honest.

Wallace fixes on a more public episode, the Chris Duren incident, when a woman stood up at one of the South Carolina town hall meetings and said her McCain-worshipping young son had been shattered when he answered the phone at their house and heard from a push-poll caller that his hero was a liar and a fraud. McCain claimed to be so devastated by this tale that he immediately announced he was pulling all his negative ads from the airwaves and called upon Bush as a fellow American to do the same. In recounting the incident, Wallace meticulously dissects the elements of sincerity and manipulation, which were marbled together like fat and muscle in a prime steak. This was too lucky a break for McCain to have just happened the spontaneous way it appeared to; his distraught reaction can't have been uninfluenced by political calculation. But ultimately, neither the credulous explanation that McCain meant every word, nor the cynical one that he manipulated the episode for political advantage, accounts for the observed facts.

Wallace homes in on this ambiguity, describing the spring of 2000 as "a moment when blunt, I-don't-give-a-shit-if-you-elect-me honesty becomes an incredibly attractive and salable and electable quality. A moment when an anticandidate can be a real candidate. But of course if he becomes a real candidate, is he still an anticandidate? Can you sell someone's refusal to be for sale?"

The spring of 2008 is surely another such moment. John McCain has taken a brave stance in defiance of his party on such issues as immigration and ethics reform, and stood his ground for what he thinks is right in Iraq, regardless of what you think. But the same McCain has surrounded himself with the worst of Washington's hired-gun lobbyists, surrendered his sound opposition to Bush's tax cuts, and groveled to the basest elements of the religious right. He winks at us, hoping that we'll bracket his compromises as ironies and not take his more politically craven moments as reflective of the true man. He can lie with dogs and not get fleas — though he openly acknowledges, such as when discussing the Keating Five scandal, that he's gotten them before. And perhaps it's not unfair that McCain sometimes gets away with what a Mitt Romney or a Hillary Clinton can't. As Bob Dole reportedly once said about one of McCain's outrageous statements: "You spend five years in a box, and you're entitled to speak your mind."

David Foster Wallace's question remains the nub of the matter—not just about John McCain, but for his likely Democratic opponent as well. In a larger sense, it's the question we ask ourselves continually through our long American election seasons. Are these guys for real? And as we try to answer, we butt up against the problem that the projection of political integrity inevitably reflects both genuine conviction and opportunistic stratagem. In a campaign, candor is always bounded by some degree of calculation. And in some cases, the display of candor is itself a canny calculation.

So which is it this time, hypocrisy or paradox? The contradictions of John McCain are upon us once again.

—Jacob Weisberg
April 16, 2008

McCain's
Promise

Optional Preface

FROM THE AD 2000 INTRODUCTION
TO THE ELECTRONIC EDITION
OF THIS WORK, MANDATED AND
OVERSEEN BY THE (NOW-DEFUNCT)
"I-PUBLISH" DIVISION OF LITTLE,
BROWN AND COMPANY, INC.

Dear Person Reading This:

Evidently I'm supposed to say something about what the following document is and where it came from.

From what I understand, in autumn 1999 the powers that be at *Rolling Stone* magazine decided they wanted to get four writers who were not political journalists to do articles on the four big presidential candidates and their day-to-day campaigns in the early primaries. My own résumé happens to have "NOT A POLITICAL JOURNALIST" right there at the very top, and *Rolling Stone* magazine called, and pitched the idea, and furthermore said I could pick whichever candidate I wanted (which of course was flattering, although in retrospect they probably told the other three writers the same thing — magazines are always very flattering and *carte blanche*ish when they're trying to get you to do something). The only candidate I could see trying to write about was Senator John McCain (R-AZ), whom I'd seen a recent tape of on *Charlie Rose* and had decided was either incredibly honest and forthright or else just insane. There were other reasons for wanting to write about McCain and party politics, too, all of which are explored in considerable detail in the document itself and so I don't see any reason to inflict them on you here.

The *Electronic Editor* (actual title, like on his office letterhead and everything) says I should insert here that I, the author, am not a Republican, and that actually I ended up voting for Sen. Bill Bradley (D-NJ) in the Illinois primary. I don't personally see how my own politics are anybody's business, but I'm guessing the point of the insertion is to make clear that there are no partisan motives or conservative agenda behind the article even though parts of it (i.e., of the upcoming article) might appear to be pro-McCain. It's not, though neither is it anti-; it's just meant to be the truth as one person saw it.

What else to tell you. At first I was supposed to follow McCain around in New Hampshire as he campaigned for 1 February's big primary there. Then, around Christmastime, *Rolling Stone* decided that they wanted to abort the assignment because Governor Bush was way ahead in the polls and outspending McCain ten to one and they thought McCain was going to get flattened in New Hampshire and that his campaign would be over by the time anything could come out in *Rolling Stone* and that they'd look stupid. Then on 1 February, when the early NH returns had McCain ahead, the magazine suddenly turned around and called again and said the article was a Go again but that now they wanted me to fly out to NH and start that very night, which (because I happen to have dogs with professionally diagnosed emotional problems who require special care, and it always takes me several days to recruit, interview, select, instruct, and field-test a dogsitter) was out of the question. Some of this is probably not too germane, but the point is that I ended up flying out the following week and riding with the McCain2000 traveling press corps from 7 to 13 February, which in retrospect was probably the most interesting and complicated week of the whole 2000 GOP race.

Especially the complicated part. For it turned out that the more interesting a campaign-related person or occurrence or intrigue or strategy or happenstance was, the more time and page-space it took to make sense of it, or, if it made no sense, to describe what it was and explain why it didn't make sense but was interesting anyway if viewed in a certain context that then itself had to be described, and so on. With the end result being that the actual document delivered per contract to *Rolling Stone* magazine turned out to be longer and more complicated than they'd asked for. Quite a bit longer, actually. In fact the article's editor pointed out that running the whole thing would take up most of *Rolling Stone*'s text-space and might even cut into the percentage of the magazine reserved for advertisements, which obviously would not do.* And so at least half the article got cut out, plus some of the more complicated stuff got way compressed and simplified, which was especially disappointing because, as previously mentioned, the most complicated stuff also tended to be the most interesting.

The point here is that what you've just now purchased the ability to download or have e-mailed to

---

* Here I should point out that this *RS* editor, whose name was Mr. Tonelli, delivered the length-and-space verdict with sympathy and good humor, and that he was pretty much a mensch through the whole radically ablative editorial process that followed, which process was itself unusually rushed and stressful because right in the middle of it (the process) came Super Tuesday's bloodbath, and McCain really did drop out—Mr. Tonelli was actually watching McCain's announcement on his office TV while we were doing the first round of cuts on the telephone—and apparently *Rolling Stone*'s top brass's

you or whatever (it's been explained to me several times, but I still don't totally understand it) is the original uncut document, the as it were director's cut, verbally complete and unoccluded by any lush photos of puffy-lipped girls with their Diesels half unzipped, etc.

There are only a couple changes. All typos and factual boners have now (hopefully) been fixed, for one thing. There were also certain places where the original article talked about the fact that it was appearing in *Rolling Stone* magazine and that whoever was reading it was sitting there actually holding a copy of *Rolling Stone*, etc., and many of these got changed because it just seemed too weird to keep telling you you were reading this in an actual 10" × 12" magazine when you now quite clearly are not. (Again, this was the Electronic Editor's suggestion.) You will note, though, that the author is usually still referred to in the document as *"Rolling Stone"* or *"RS."* I'm sorry if this looks strange to you, but I have declined

---

fear of looking stupid came roaring back into their limbic system and they told poor Mr. Tonelli that the article had to be all of a sudden crammed into the very next issue of *RS,* even though that issue was scheduled to "close" and go to the printer in less than 48 hours, which, if you know anything about magazines' normally interminable editing and fact-checking and copyediting and typesetting and proofreading and retypesetting and layout and printing processes, you'll understand why Mr. Tonelli's good humor through the whole thing was noteworthy.

to change it. Part of the reason is that I was absurdly proud of my *Rolling Stone* press badge and of the fact that most of the pencils and campaign staff referred to me as "the guy from *Rolling Stone.*" I will confess that I even borrowed a friend's battered old black leather jacket to wear on the Trail so I'd better project the kind of edgy, vaguely dangerous vibe I imagined an *RS* reporter ought to give off. (You have to understand that I hadn't read *Rolling Stone* in quite some time.) Plus, journalistically, my covering the campaign for this particular organ turned out to have a big effect on what I got to see and how various people conducted themselves when I was around. For example, it was the main reason why the McCain2000 High Command pretty much refused to have anything to do with me* but why the network techs were so friendly and forthcoming and let me hang around with them (the sound techs, in particular, were *Rolling Stone* fans from way back). Finally, the document itself is sort of rhetorically directed at

---

* In particular I never got to talk to Mr. Mike Murphy, who if you read the document you'll understand why he'd be the one McCain staffer you'd just about give a nut to get three or four drinks into and then start probing. Despite sustained pestering and sleeve-tugging and pride-swallowing appeals to the Head Press Liaison for even just ten lousy minutes, though—and even after *RS*'s Mr. Tonelli himself called McCain2000 HQ in Virginia to bitch and wheedle—Mike Murphy avoided this reporter to the point of actually starting to duck around corners whenever he saw me coming. The unending pursuit of this one interview (what eventually in my notebook got called

voters of a particular age-range and attitude, and I'm figuring that the occasional *Rolling Stone* reference might help keep the reasons for some of this rhetoric clear.

The other thing I'd note is simply what the article's about, which turned out to be not so much the campaign of one impressive guy, but rather what McCain's candidacy and the brief weird excitement it generated might reveal about how millennial politics and all its packaging and marketing and strategy and media and spin and general sepsis actually makes us US voters feel, inside, and whether anyone running for anything can even be "real" anymore — whether what we actually want is something real or something

---

"*MurphyQuest 2000*") actually turned into one of the great personal subdramas of the week, and there's a whole very lengthy and sordid story to tell here, including some embarrassing but probably in retrospect kind of funny attempts to corner the poor man in all sorts of awkward personal venues where I figured he'd have a hard time escaping... nevertheless the crux here is that Murphy's total inaccessibility to yrs. truly was not, I finally realized, anything personal, but rather a simple function of my being from *Rolling Stone*, a (let's face it) politically featherweight organ whose readership was clearly not part of any GOP demographic that was going to help Mike Murphy's candidate in SC or MI or any of the other upcoming sink-or-swim primaries. In fact, because the magazine was a biweekly with a long lead time — the Lebanese-Australian lady from the *Boston Globe* (see document) pointed all this out to yrs. truly after we'd just watched Murphy more or less fake an epileptic seizure to get out of riding in an elevator with me — even a droolingly pro-McCain *Rolling Stone* article wouldn't actually appear until after 7 March's Super Tuesday, by which time, she predicted (correctly), the nomination battle would effectively be over.

else. Whether it works on your screen or Palm or not, for me the whole thing ended up relevant in ways far beyond any one man or magazine. If you don't agree, I imagine you'll have only to press a button or two to make it all go away.

Who Cares

All right so now yes yes *more* press attention for John S. McCain III, USN, POW, USC, GOP, 2000.com. The Rocky of Politics. The McCain Mutiny. The Real McCain. The Straight Talk Express. Internet fundraiser. Media darling. Navy flier. Middle name Sidney. Son and grandson of admirals. And a serious hardass—a way-Right Republican senator from one of the most politically troglodytic states in the nation. A man who opposes *Roe v. Wade,* gun control, and funding for PBS, who supports the death penalty and defense buildups and constitutional amendments outlawing flag-burning and making school prayer OK. Who voted to convict at Clinton's impeachment trial, twice. And who, starting sometime last fall, has become the great populist hope of American politics. Who wants your vote but won't whore himself to get it, and wants you to vote for him *because* he won't whore. An anticandidate. Who cares.

Facts. The 1996 presidential election had the lowest Young Voter turnout in US history. The 2000 GOP primary in New Hampshire had the highest. And the experts agree that McCain drew most of them. He drew first-time and never-before voters; he drew Democrats and Independents, Libertarians and soft socialists and college kids and soccer moms and weird furtive guys whose affiliations sounded more like cells than parties, and won by 18 points, and nearly wiped the smirk off Bush$_2$'s face. McCain has spurned soft money and bundled money and still raised millions, much of it on the Internet and from people who've never given to a campaign before. On 7 Feb. '00 he's on the cover of all three major newsweeklies at once, and the Shrub is on the run. The next big vote is South Carolina, heart of the true knuckle-dragging Christian Right, where Dixie's flag flutters proud over the statehouse and the favorite sport is video poker and the state GOP is getting sued over its habit of not even opening polls in black areas on primary day; and when McCain's chartered plane lands here at 0300h on the night of his New Hampshire win, a good 500 South Carolina college students are waiting to greet him, cheering and waving signs and dancing and holding a weird kind of GOP rave. Think about this—500 kids at 3:00 AM out of their minds with enthusiasm for…a politician. "It was as if," *Time* said, "[McCain] were on the cover of *Rolling Stone*," giving the rave all kinds of attention.

And of course attention breeds attention, as any marketer can tell you. And so now more attention, from the aforementioned ur-liberal *Rolling Stone* itself, whose editors send the least professional pencil they can find to spend a week on the campaign with McCain and *Time* and the *Times* and CNN and

MSNBC and MTV and all the rest of this country's great digital engine of public fuss. Does John McCain deserve all this? Is the attention real attention, or just hype? Is there a difference? Can it help him get elected? Should it?

A better question: Do you even give a shit whether McCain can or ought to win. Since you're reading *Rolling Stone,* the chances are good that you are an American between say 18 and 35, which demographically makes you a Young Voter. And no generation of Young Voters has ever cared less about politics and politicians than yours. There's hard demographic and voter-pattern data backing this up…assuming you give a shit about data. In fact, even if you're reading other stuff in *RS,* the odds are probably only about 50-50 that you'll read this whole document once you've seen what it's really about—such is the enormous shuddering yawn that the political process tends to evoke in us now in this post-Watergate-post-Iran-Contra-post-Whitewater-post-Lewinsky era, an era in which politicians' statements of principle or vision are understood as self-serving ad copy and judged not for their truth or ability to inspire but for their tactical shrewdness, their marketability. And no generation has been marketed and spun and pitched to as relentlessly as today's demographic Young. So when Senator John McCain says, in Michigan or SC, "I run for president not to Be Somebody, but to Do Something," it's hard to hear it as anything more than a marketing tactic, especially when he says it as he's going around surrounded by cameras and reporters and cheering crowds...in other words, Being Somebody.

And when Senator John McCain also says—constantly, thumping it hard at the start and end of every speech and Town Hall Meeting—that his goal as president will be "to inspire young Americans to devote themselves to causes greater than their own self-interest," it's hard not to hear it as just one more piece of the carefully scripted bullshit that presidential candidates hand us as they go about the self-interested business of trying to become the most powerful, important, and talked-about human being on earth, which is of course their real "cause," a cause to which they appear to be so deeply devoted that they can swallow and spew whole mountains of noble-sounding bullshit and convince even themselves they mean it. Cynical as that may sound, polls show it's how most of us feel. And we're beyond not believing the bullshit; mostly we don't even *hear* it now, dismissing it at the same deep level, below attention, where we also block out billboards and Muzak.

One of the things that makes John McCain's "causes greater than self-interest" line harder to dismiss, though, is that this guy also sometimes says things that are manifestly true but which no other mainstream candidate will say. Such as that special-interest money, billions of dollars of it, controls Washington and that all this "reforming politics" and "cleaning up Washington" stuff that every candidate talks about will remain impossible until certain well-known campaign-finance scams like soft money and bundles are outlawed. All Congress's talk about health-care reform and a Patients' Bill of Rights, for example, McCain has said publicly is total bullshit because the GOP is in the pocket of pharmaceutical and HMO lobbies and the Democrats are funded by trial lawyers' lobbies, and it is in these backers' self-interest to see that the current insane US health-care system stays just the way it is.

But health-care reform is politics, and so are marginal tax rates and defense procurement and Social Security, and politics is boring—complex, abstract, dry, the province of policy wonks and Rush Limbaugh and nerdy little guys on PBS, and basically who cares.

Except there's something underneath politics here, something riveting and unspinnable and true. It has to do with McCain's military background and Vietnam combat and the 5+ years he spent in a North Vietnamese prison, mostly in solitary, in a box-sized cell, getting tortured and starved. And with the unbelievable honor and balls he showed there. It's very easy to gloss over the POW thing, partly because we've all heard so much about it and partly because it's so off-the-charts dramatic, like something in a movie

instead of a man's real life. But it's worth considering for a minute, carefully, because it's what makes
McCain's "causes greater than self-interest" thing
easier to maybe swallow.

Here's what happened. In October of '67 McCain
was himself still a Young Voter and was flying his 26th
Vietnam combat mission and his A-4 Skyhawk plane
got shot down over Hanoi, and he had to eject, which
basically means setting off an explosive charge that
blows your seat out of the plane, and the ejection
broke both McCain's arms and one leg and gave him
a concussion and he started falling out of the skies
over Hanoi. Try to imagine for a second how much
this would hurt and how scared you'd be, three limbs
broken and falling toward the enemy capital you just
tried to bomb. His chute opened late and he landed
hard in a little lake in a park right in the middle of
downtown Hanoi. (There is still an NV statue of
McCain by this lake today, showing him on his knees
with his hands up and eyes scared and on the pedi-
ment the inscription "McCan—famous air pirate"
[*sic*].) Imagine treading water with broken arms and
trying to pull the life vest's toggle with your teeth as a
crowd of North Vietnamese men all swim out toward
you (there's film of this, somebody had a home-movie
camera and the NV government released it, though
it's grainy and McCain's face is hard to see). The
crowd pulled him out and then just about killed him.

Bomber pilots were especially hated, for obvious reasons. McCain got bayoneted in the groin; a soldier broke his shoulder apart with a rifle butt. Plus by this time his right knee was bent 90 degrees to the side, with the bone sticking out. This is all public record. Try to imagine it. He finally got tossed on a jeep and taken only about five blocks to the infamous Hoa Lo prison—a.k.a. the Hanoi Hilton, of much movie fame—where for a week they made him beg for a doctor and finally set a couple of the fractures without anesthetic and let two other fractures and the groin wound (imagine: *groin wound*) go untreated. Then they threw him in a cell. Try for a moment to feel this. The media profiles all talk about how McCain still can't lift his arms over his head to comb his hair, which is true. But try to imagine it at the time, yourself in his place, because it's important. Think about how *diametrically* opposed to your own self-interest getting knifed in the nuts and having fractures set without a general would be, and then about getting thrown in a cell to just lie there and hurt, which is what happened. He was mostly delirious with pain for weeks, and his weight dropped to 100 pounds, and the other POWs were sure he would die; and then, after he'd hung on like that for several months and his bones had mostly knitted and he could sort of stand up, the prison people came and brought him to the commandant's office and closed the door and out of nowhere offered to let him go. They said he could just…leave. It turned out that US Admiral John S. McCain II had just been made head of all naval forces in the Pacific, meaning also Vietnam, and the North Vietnamese wanted the PR coup of mercifully releasing his son, the baby-killer. And John S. McCain III, 100 pounds and barely able to stand, refused the offer. The US military's Code of Conduct for Prisoners of War apparently said that POWs had to be released in the order they were captured, and there were others who'd been in Hoa Lo a much longer time, and McCain refused to violate the Code. The prison commandant, not at all pleased, right there in his office had guards break McCain's ribs, rebreak his arm, knock his teeth out. McCain still refused to leave without the other POWs. Forget how many movies stuff like this happens in and try to imagine it as real: a man without teeth refusing release. McCain spent four more years in Hoa Lo like this, much of the time in solitary, in the dark, in a special closet-sized box called a "punishment cell." Maybe you've heard all this before; it's been in umpteen different media profiles of McCain this year. It's overexposed, true. Still, though, take a second or two to do some creative visualization and imagine the moment between John McCain's first getting offered early release and his turning it down. Try to imagine it was you. Imagine how loudly your most basic, primal self-interest would cry out to you in that moment, and

all the ways you could rationalize accepting the offer:
What difference would one less POW make? Plus
maybe it'd give the other POWs hope and keep them
going, and I mean 100 pounds and expected to die
and surely the Code of Conduct doesn't apply to you
if you need a doctor or else you're going to die, plus
if you could stay alive by getting out you could make
a promise to God to do nothing but Total Good from
now on and make the world better and so your accepting would be better for the world than your refusing,
and maybe if Dad wasn't worried about the Vietnamese retaliating against you here in prison he could
prosecute the war more aggressively and end it sooner
and actually save lives so yes maybe you could actually
save lives if you took the offer and got out versus what
real purpose gets served by you staying here in a box
and getting beaten to death, and by the way oh Jesus
imagine it a real doctor and real surgery with pain-
killers and clean sheets and a chance to heal and not
be in agony and to see your kids again, your wife, to
smell your wife's hair....Can you hear it? What would
be happening inside your head? Would you have
refused the offer? *Could* you have? You can't know for
sure. None of us can. It's hard even to imagine the lev-
els of pain and fear and want in that moment, much
less to know how we'd react. None of us can know.

But, see, we *do* know how this man reacted. That he
chose to spend four more years there, mostly in a dark

box, alone, tapping messages on the walls to the others, rather than violate a Code. Maybe he was nuts. But the point is that with McCain it feels like we *know,* for a proven fact, that he is capable of devotion to something other, more, than his own self-interest. So that when he says the line in speeches now you can feel like maybe it's not just more candidate bullshit, that with this guy it's maybe the truth. Or maybe both the truth *and* bullshit—the man does want your vote, after all.

But so that moment in the Hoa Lo office in '68—right before John McCain refused, with all his basic primal human self-interest howling at him—that moment is hard to blow off. For the whole week, through Michigan and South Carolina and all the tedium and cynicism and paradox of the campaign, that moment seems to underlie McCain's "greater than self-interest" line, moor it, give it a deep sort of reverb that's hard to ignore. The fact is that John McCain is a genuine hero of maybe the only kind Vietnam has to offer us, a hero because of not what he did but what he suffered—voluntarily, for a Code. This gives him the moral authority both to utter lines about causes beyond self-interest and to expect us, even in this age of spin and lawyerly cunning, to believe he means them. And yes, literally: "moral authority," that old cliché, like so many other clichés—"service," "honor," "duty"—that have become now just mostly words, slogans invoked by men in nice suits who want something from us. The

John McCain of recent seasons, though—arguing for his doomed campaign-finance bill on the Senate floor in '98, calling his colleagues crooks to their faces on C-SPAN, talking openly about a bought-and-paid-for government on *Charlie Rose* in July '99, unpretentious and bright as hell in the Iowa debates and New Hampshire THMs—something about him made a lot of us feel that the guy wanted something different from us, something more than votes or dollars, something old and maybe corny but with a weird achy pull to it like a smell from childhood or a name on the tip of your tongue, something that would make us hear clichés as more than just clichés and start us trying to think about what terms like "service" and "sacrifice" and "honor" might really refer to, like whether the words actually *stand* for something. To think about whether anything past well-spun self-interest might be real, was ever real, and if so then what happened? These, for the most part, are not lines of thinking that our culture has encouraged Young Voters to pursue. Why do you suppose that is?

Glossary of Relevant Campaign Trail Vocab, Mostly Courtesy of Jim C. and the Network News Techs

22.5 = The press corps' shorthand for McCain's opening remarks at *THMs* (see *THM*), which remarks are always the same and always take exactly 22½ minutes.

B-film = Innocuous little audio-free shots of McCain doing public stuff—shaking hands, signing books, getting *scrummed* (see *Scrum*), etc.—for use behind a TV voice-over report on the day's campaigning, as in "The reason the *techs* [see *Tech*] have to *feed* [see *Feed*] so much irrelevant and repetitive daily footage is that they never know what the network wants to use for *B-film.*"

Baggage Call = The grotesquely early AM time, listed on the next day's schedule (N.B.: the last vital media-task of the day is making sure to get the next day's schedule from Travis), by which you have to get your suitcase back in the bus's bowels and have a seat staked out and be ready to go or else you get left behind and have to try to wheedle a ride to the first *THM* (see *THM*) from FoxNews, which is a drag in all kinds of ways.

Bundled Money = A way to get around the Federal Election Commission's $1,000 limit for individual campaign contributions. A wealthy donor can give $1,000 for himself, then he can say that yet another $1,000 comes from his wife, and another $1,000 from his kid, and another from his Aunt Edna, etc. The *Shrub*'s (see *Shrub*) favorite trick is to designate CEOs and other top corporate executives as "Pioneers," each of whom pledges to raise $100,000 for Bush2000—$1,000 comes from them individually, and the other 99 one-grand contributions come "voluntarily" from their employees. McCain makes a point of accepting neither b*undled money* nor s*oft money* (see *Soft Money*).

Cabbage (v) = To beg, divert, or outright steal food from one of the many suppertime campaign events at which McCain's audience all sit at tables and get supper and the press corps has to stand around foodless at the back of the room.

DT = Drive Time, the slots in the daily schedule set aside for caravanning from one campaign event to another.

F&F – An hour or two in the afternoon when the campaign provides downtime and an *F&F* Room for the press corps to *file* and *feed* (see *File* and *Feed*).

File and *Feed* = What print and broadcast press, respectively, have to do every day, i.e., print reporters have to finish their daily stories and *file* them via fax or e-mail to their newspapers, while the *techs* (see *Tech*) and field producers have to find a satellite or *Gunner* (see *Gunner*) and *feed* their film, *B-film, stand-ups* (see *Stand-up*), and anything else their bosses might want to the network HQ. (For alternate meaning of *feed*, see *Pool*.)

Gunner = A portable satellite-uplink rig that the networks use to *feed* on-scene from some campaign events. Gunner is the company that makes and/or rents out these rigs, which consist of a blinding white van with a boat-trailerish thing on which is an eight-foot satellite dish angled 40 degrees upward at the southwest sky and emblazoned in fiery blue caps **GUNNER GLOBAL UPLINKING FOR NEWS, NETWORKING, ENTERTAINMENT.**

Head = Local or network TV correspondent (see also *Talent*).

ODT = Optimistic Drive Time, which refers to the daily schedule's nagging habit of underestimating the amount of time it takes to get from one event to another, causing the Straight Talk Express driver to speed like a maniac and thereby to incur the rabid dislike of Jay and the Bullshit 2 driver. (On the night of 9 February, one BS2 driver actually quit on the spot after an especially hair-rising ride from Greenville to Clemson U, and an emergency replacement driver [who wore a brown cowboy hat with two NRA pins on the brim and was so obsessed with fuel economy that he refused ever to turn on BS2's generator, causing all BS2 press who needed working AC outlets to crowd onto BS1 and turning BS2 into a veritable moving tomb used only for *OTC*s] had to be flown in from Cincinnati, which is apparently the bus company's HQ.)

OTC = Opportunity to Crash, meaning a chance to grab a nap on the bus (placement and posture variable).

OTS = Opportunity to Smoke.

Pencil = A member of the Trail's print press.

Pool (*v*) = Refers to occasions when, because of space restrictions or McCain2000 fiat, only one network camera-and-sound team is allowed into an event, and by convention all the other networks get to *feed* (meaning, in this case, *pool*) that one team's tape.

Press-Avail (or just *Avail*) = Brief scheduled opportunity for traveling press corps to interface as one body w/ McCain or staff High Command, often deployed for *Reacts* (see *React*). An *Avail* is less formal than a press conference, which latter usually draws extra local *pencils* and *heads* and is uncancelable, whereas *Avails* are often bagged because of *ODTs* and related snafus.

React (*n*) = McCain's or McCain2000 High Command's on-record response to a sudden major development in the campaign, usually some tactical move or allegation from the *Shrub* (see *Shrub*).

Scrum (*n*) = The moving 360-degree ring of *techs* (see *Tech*) and *heads* around a candidate as he makes his way from the Straight Talk Express into an event or vice versa; (*v*) = to gather around a moving candidate in such a ring.

Shrub = GOP presidential candidate George W. Bush (also sometimes referred to as Dubya or Bush$_2$).

Soft Money = The best-known way to finesse the

FEC's limit on campaign contributions. Enormous sums are here given to a certain candidate's political party instead of to the candidate, but the party then by some strange coincidence ends up disbursing those enormous sums to exactly the candidate the donor had wanted to give to in the first place.

Stand-up = A *head* doing a remote report from some event McCain's at.

Stick = A sound *tech*'s (see *Tech*) black telescoping polymer rod (full extension = 9'7") with a boom microphone at the end, used mostly for *scrums* and always the most distinctive visible feature thereof because of the way a fully extended *stick* wobbles and boings when the sound *tech* (which, again, see *Tech*) walks with it.

Talent = A marquee network *head* who flies in for just one day, gets briefed by a field producer, and does a *stand-up* on the campaign, as in "We got *talent* coming in tomorrow, so I need to get all this *B-film* archived." Recognizable *talent* this week includes Bob Schieffer of CBS, David Bloom of NBC, and Judy Woodruff of CNN.

Tech = A TV news camera or sound technician. (N.B.: In the McCain corps this week, all the *techs* are male, while over 80 percent of the field producers are female. No credible explanation ever obtained.)

THM = Town Hall Meeting, McCain2000's signature campaign event, where the *22.5* is followed by an hour-long unscreened Q&A with the audience.

The Twelve Monkeys (or *12M*) = The *techs'* private code-name for the most elite and least popular *pencils* in the McCain press corps, who on *DTs* are almost always allowed into the red-intensive salon at the very back of the Straight Talk Express to interface with McCain and political consultant Mike Murphy. The *12M* are a dozen high-end journalists and political-analysis guys from important papers and weeklies and news services (e.g. Copley, *W. Post, WSJ, Newsweek,* UPI, *Ch. Tribune, National Review, Atlanta Constitution,* etc.) and tend to be so totally identical in dress and demeanor as to be almost surreal — twelve immaculate and wrinkle-free navy-blue blazers, half-Windsored ties, pleated chinos, oxfordcloth shirts that even when the jackets come off stay 100 percent buttoned at collar and sleeves, Cole Haan loafers, and tortoiseshell specs they love to take off and nibble the arm of, plus a uniform self-seriousness that reminds you of every overachieving dweeb you ever wanted to kick the ass of in school. The *Twelve Monkeys* never smoke or drink, and always move in a pack, and always cut to the front of every *scrum* and *Press-Avail* and line for continental breakfast in the hotel lobby before *Baggage Call,* and whenever any of them are rotated briefly back onto Bullshit 1 they always sit together identically huffy and pigeon-toed with their attaché cases in their laps and always end up discussing esoteric books on political theory and public policy in voices that are all the exact same plummy Ivy League honk. The *techs* (who wear old jeans and surplus-store parkas and also all tend to hang in a pack) pretty much try to ignore the *Twelve Monkeys,* who in turn treat the *techs* the way someone in an executive washroom treats the attendant. As you might already have gathered, *Rolling Stone* dislikes the *12M* intensely, for all the above reasons, plus the fact that they're tight as the bark on a tree when it comes to sharing even very basic general-knowledge political information that might help somebody write a slightly better article, plus the issue of two separate occasions at late-night hotel check-ins when one or more of the *Twelve Monkeys* just out of nowhere turned and handed *Rolling Stone* their suitcases to carry, as if *Rolling Stone* were a bellboy or gofer instead of a hardworking journalist just like them even if he didn't have a portable Paul Stuart steamer for his slacks.

Weasel = The weird gray fuzzy thing that sound *techs* put over their *sticks'* mikes at *scrums* to keep annoying wind-noise off the audio. It looks like a large floppy mouse-colored version of a certain popular kind of fuzzy bathroom slipper. (N.B.: *Weasels,* which are also sometimes worn by sound *techs* as headgear during *OTS*s when it's really cold, are thus sometimes also known as *tech toupees.*)

Substantially Farther
Behind the Scenes
than You're Apt to Want to Be

It's now precisely 1330h on Tuesday, 8 February 2000, on Bullshit 1, proceeding southeast on I-26 back toward Charleston SC. There's now so much press and staff and techs and stringers and field producers and photographers and heads and pencils and political columnists and hosts of political radio shows and local media covering John McCain and the McCain2000 phenomenon that there's more than one campaign bus. Here in South Carolina there are three, a veritable convoy of Straight Talk, plus FoxNews's green SUV and the MTV crew's sprightly red Corvette and two much-antenna'd local TV vans (one of which has muffler trouble). On DTs like this, McCain's always in his personal red recliner next to pol. consultant Mike Murphy's red recliner in the little press salon he and Murphy have in the back of the lead bus, the well-known Straight Talk Express, which is up ahead and already drawing away. The Straight Talk Express's driver is a leadfoot and the other drivers hate him. Bullshit 1 is the caravan's second bus, a luxury Grumman with good current and workable phone jacks, and a lot of the national pencils use it to pound out copy on their laptops and send faxes and e-mail stuff to their editors. The campaign's logistics are dizzyingly complex, and one of the things the McCain2000 staff has to do is rent different buses and decorate the nicest one with STRAIGHT TALK EXPRESS and McCAIN2000.COM in each new state. In Michigan yesterday there was just the STE plus one bus for non-elite press, which had powder-gray faux-leather couches and gleaming brushed-steel fixtures and a mirrored ceiling from front to back; it creeped everyone out and was christened the Pimpmobile. The two press buses in South Carolina are known as Bullshit 1 and Bullshit 2, names conceived as usual by the extremely cool and laid-back NBC News cameraman Jim C. and—to their credit—immediately seized on and used with great glee at every opportunity by McCain's younger Press Liaisons, who are themselves so cool and unpretentious it's tempting to suspect that they are *professionally* cool and unpretentious.

Right now Bullshit 1's Press Liaison, Travis—23, late of Georgetown U and a six-month backpack tour of Southeast Asia during which he says he came to like fried bugs—is again employing his single most important and impressive skill as a McCain2000 staffer, which is the ability to sleep anywhere, anytime, and in any position for ten-to-fifteen-minute intervals, with a composed face and no unpleasant sounds or fluids, and then to come instantly and unfuzzily awake the moment he's needed. It's not clear whether he thinks people can't tell he's sleeping or what. Travis, who wears wide-wale corduroys and a sweater from Structure and seems to subsist entirely on Starburst Fruit Chews, tends to speak with the same deprecatory irony that is the whole staff's style, introducing himself to new media today as either "Your press lackey" or "The Hervé Villechaize of Bullshit 1," or both. His latest trick is to go up to the front of the bus and hook his arm over the little brushed-steel safety bar above the driver's head and to lean against it so that from behind it looks as if he's having an involved navigational conversation with the driver, and to go to sleep, and the driver—a 6'7" bald black gentleman named Jay, whose way of saying goodnight to a journalist at the end of the day is "Go on and get you a woman, boy!"—knows exactly what's going on and takes extra care not to change lanes or brake hard, and Travis, whose day starts at 0500 and ends after midnight just like all the other staffers, lives this way.

McCain just got done giving a Major Policy Address on crime and punishment at the South Carolina Criminal Justice Academy in Columbia, which is where the caravan is heading back to Charleston from. It was a resoundingly scary speech, delivered in a large airless cinderblock auditorium surrounded by razor wire and guard towers (the SCCJA adjoined a penal institution so closely that it wasn't clear where one left off and the other began) and introduced by some kind of very high-ranking Highway Patrol officer whose big hanging gut and face the color of rare steak seemed right out of southern-law-enforcement central casting and who spoke approvingly and at some length about Senator McCain's military background and his 100 percent conservative voting record on crime, punishment, firearms, and the war on drugs. This wasn't a Town Meeting Q&A–type thing; it was a Major Policy Address, one of three this week prompted by Bush2000's charges that McCain is fuzzy on policy, that he's image over substance. The speech's putative audience was 350 neckless young men and women sitting at attention (if that's possible) in arrow-straight rows of folding chairs, with another couple hundred law enforcement pros in Highway Patrol hats and mirrored shades standing at parade-rest behind them, and then behind and around them the media—the real audience for the speech—including NBC's Jim C. and his soundman Frank C. (no relation) and the rest of the network techs on the ever-present fiberboard riser facing the stage and filming McCain, who as is SOP first thanks a whole lot of local people nobody's heard of and then w/o ado jumps right into what's far and away the most frightening speech of the week, backed as always by a 30' × 50' American flag so that when you see B-film of these things on TV it's McCain and the flag, the flag and McCain, a visual conjunction all the candidates try to hammer home.

The seated cadets—none of whom fidget or scratch or move in any way except to blink in what looks like perfect sync—wear identical dark-brown khakis and junior models of the same round big-brimmed hats their elders wear, so that they look like ten perfect rows of brutal and extremely attentive forest rangers. McCain, who does not ever perspire, is wearing a dark suit and wide tie and has the only dry forehead in the hall. US congressmen Lindsey Graham (R-SC, of impeachment-trial fame) and Mark Sanford (R-SC, rated the single most fiscally conservative member of the '98–'00 Congress) are up there onstage behind McCain, as is also SOP; they're sort of his living letters of introduction down here this week. Graham, as usual, looks like he slept in his suit, whereas Sanford is tan and urbane in a V-neck sweater and Guccis whose shine you could read by. Mrs. Cindy McCain is up there too, brittly composed and smiling at the air in front of her and thinking about God knows what. Half the buses' press don't listen to the speech; most of them are at different spots at the very back of the auditorium, walking in little unconscious circles with their cellular phones. (You should be apprised up front that national reporters spend an enormous amount of time either on their cell phones or waiting for their cell phones to ring. It is not an exaggeration to say that when somebody's cell phone breaks they almost have to be sedated.) The techs for CBS,

NBC, CNN, ABC, and Fox will film the whole speech plus any remarks afterward, then they'll unbolt their cameras from the tripods and go mobile and scrum McCain's exit and the brief Press-Avail at the door to the Straight Talk Express, and then the field producers will call network HQ and summarize the highlights and HQ will decide which five- or ten-second snippet gets used for their news's nightly bit on the GOP campaign.

It helps to conceive a campaign week's events in terms of boxes, boxes inside other boxes, etc. The national voting audience is the great huge outer box, then the SC-electorate audience, mediated respectively by the inner layers of national and local press, just inside which lie the insulating boxes of McCain's staff's High Command who plan and stage events and spin stuff for the layers of press to interpret for the layers of audience, and the Press Liaisons who shepherd the pencils and heads and mediate their access to the High Command and control which media get rotated onto the ST Express (which is itself a box in motion) and then decide (the Liaisons do) which of these chosen media then get to move all the way into the extreme rear's salon to interface with McCain himself, who is the campaign's narrator and narrative at once, a candidate whose biggest draw of course is that he's an anticandidate, someone who's open and accessible and "thinks outside the box," but who is in fact

the campaign's Chinese boxes' central and inscrutable core box, and whose own intracranial thoughts on
all these boxes and layers and lenses and on whether
this new kind of enclosure is anything like Hoa Lo's
dark box are pretty much anyone in the media's guess,
since all he'll talk about is politics.

Plus Bullshit 1 is also a box, of course, just the way
anything you can't exit till somebody else lets you out
is, and right now there are 27 members of the national
political media on board, halfway to Charleston. A
certain percentage of them aren't worth introducing
you to because they'll get rotated back off the Trail
tonight and be gone tomorrow, replaced by others
you'll just be starting to recognize by the time they too
rotate out. That's what these pros call it, the Trail, the
same way musicians talk about the Road. The schedule is fascist: wake-up call and backup alarm at 0600h,
express check-out, Baggage Call at 0700 to throw bags
and techs' gear under the bus, haul ass to McCain's
first THM at 0800, then another, then another, maybe
an hour off to F&F someplace if ODTs permit, then
usually two big evening events, plus hours of dead
highway DT between functions, finally getting into
that night's Marriott or Hampton Inn at like 2300 just
when room service closes so that you're begging rides
from FoxNews to find a restaurant still open, then an
hour at the hotel bar to try to shut your head off so
you can hit the rack at 0130 and get up at 0600 and

do it all again. Usually it's four to six days for the average pencil and then you go off home on a gurney and your editor rotates in fresh meat. The network techs, who are old hands at the Trail, stay on for months at a time. The McCain2000 staff have all been doing this full-time since Labor Day, and even the young ones look like the walking dead. Only McCain seems to thrive. He's 63 and practically Rockette-kicks onto the Express every morning. It's either inspiring or frightening.

Here's a quick behind-the-scenes tour of everything that's happening on BS1 at 1330h. A few of the press are slumped over sleeping, open-mouthed and twitching, using their topcoats for pillows. The CBS and NBC techs are in their usual place on the couches way up front, their cameras and sticks and boom mikes and boxes of tapes and big Duracells piled around them, discussing obscure stand-up comedians of the early 70s and trading press badges from New Hampshire and Iowa and Delaware, which badges are laminated and worn around the neck on nylon cords and apparently have value for collectors. Jim C., who looks like a chronically sleep-deprived Elliott Gould, is also watching Travis's leather bookbag swing metronomically by its over-shoulder strap as Travis leans against the safety bar and dozes. All the couches and padded chairs face in, perpendicular to BS1's length, instead of a regular bus's forward-facing seats. So everyone's legs are always out in the aisle, but there's none of the normal social anxiety about your leg maybe touching somebody else on a bus's leg because nobody can help it and everyone's too tired to care. Right behind each set of couches are small white plastic tables with recessed cup-receptacles and AC outlets that work if Jay can be induced to turn on the generator (which he will unless he's low on fuel); and the left side's table has two pencils and two field producers at it, and one of the pencils is Alison Mitchell, as in *the* Alison Mitchell, who is the *NY Times*'s daily eye on McCain and a very high-end journalist but not (refreshingly) one of the Twelve Monkeys, a slim calm kindly lady of maybe 45 who wears dark tights, pointy boots, a black sweater that looks home-crocheted, and a perpetual look of concerned puzzlement, as if life were one long request for clarification. Alison Mitchell is usually a regular up on the Straight Talk Express but today has a tight 1500h deadline and is using BS1's superior current to whip out the story on her Apple PowerBook. (Even from outside the bus it's easy to tell who's banging away on a laptop right then, because their window shades are always down against daytime glare, which is every laptop-journalist's great nemesis.) An ABC field producer across the table from A. Mitchell is trying to settle a credit card dispute on his distinctive cell phone, which is not a headset phone per se but consists of an earplug and a tiny hanging podular

thing he holds to his mouth with two fingers to speak,
a device that manages to make him look simultane-
ously deaf and schizophrenic. People in both seats
behind the table are reading *USA Today* (and this
might be worth noting — the only news daily read by
every single member of the national campaign press
is, believe it or not, *USA Today,* which always appears
as if by dark magic under everybody's hotel door
with their express check-out bill every morning, and
is free, and media are as susceptible to shrewd marketing as anybody else). The local TV truck's muffler
gets louder the farther back you go. About two-thirds
of the way down the aisle is a little area that has the
bus's refrigerator and the liquor cabinets (the latter
unbelievably well stocked on yesterday's Pimpmobile,
totally empty on BS1) and the bathroom with the hazardous door. There's also a little counter area piled
with Krispy Kreme doughnut boxes, and a sink whose
water nobody ever uses (for what turn out to be good
reasons). Krispy Kremes are sort of the Deep South
equivalent of Dunkin' Donuts, ubiquitous and cheap
and great in a sort of what-am-I-doing-eating-dessert-
for-breakfast way, and are a cornerstone of what Jim
C. calls the Campaign Diet.

Behind the buses' digestive areas is another little
lounge, which up on the Express serves as McCain's
press salon but which on Bullshit 1 is just an ellip-
tic table of beige plastic ringed with a couch it's just

a bit too high for, plus a fax machine and multiple jacks and outlets, the whole area known to the Press Liaisons as the ERPP (=Extreme Rear Press Palace). Right now Mrs. McCain's personal assistant on the Trail, Wendy—who has electric-blue contact lenses and rigid blond hair and immaculate makeup and accessories and French nails and can perhaps best be described as a very Republican-looking young lady indeed—is back here at the beige table eating a large styrofoam cup of soup and using her cell phone to try to find someplace in downtown Charleston where Mrs. McCain can get her nails done. All three walls in the ERPP are mirrored, an unsettling echo of yesterday's reflective bus (except here the mirrors have weird little white ghostly shapes embedded in the plate, apparently as decorations), so that you can see not only everybody's reflections but all sorts of multi-angled reflections of those reflections, and so on, which on top of all the jouncing and swaying keeps most folks up front despite the ERPP's wealth of facilities. Just why Wendy is arranging for her mistress's manicure here on Bullshit 1 is unclear, but Mrs. McC.'s sedulous attention to her own person's dress and grooming is already a minor legend among the press corps, and some of the techs speculate that things like getting her nails and hair done, together with being almost Siametically attached to Ms. Lisa Graham Keegan (who is AZ's education superintendent and supposedly traveling with the senator as his "Advisor on Issues Affecting Education" but is quite plainly really along because she's Cindy McCain's friend and confidante and the one person in whose presence Mrs. McC. doesn't look like a jacklighted deer), are the only things keeping this extremely fragile person together on the Trail, where she's required to stand under hot lights next to McCain at every speech and THM and Press-Avail and stare cheerfully into the middle distance while her husband speaks to crowds and lenses—in fact some of the cable-network techs have a sort of running debate about what Cindy McCain's really looking at as she stands onstage being scrutinized but never getting to say anything...and anyway, everybody understands and respects the enormous pressure Wendy's under to help Mrs. McC. keep it together, and nobody makes fun of her for things like getting more and more stressed as it becomes obvious that there's some special Southeast idiom for manicure that Wendy doesn't know, because nobody she talks to on the cell phone seems to have any idea what she means by "manicure." Also back here, directly across from Wendy, is a ridiculously handsome guy in a green cotton turtleneck, a photographer for Reuters, sitting disconsolate in a complex nest of wires plugged into just about every jack in the ERPP; he's got digital photos of the Columbia speech in his Toshiba laptop and has his cell phone plugged into both the wall and the laptop (which is itself plugged into the wall) and is trying to file the pictures via some weird inter-Reuters e-mail, except his laptop has decided it doesn't like his cell phone anymore ("like" = his term), and he can't get it to file.

If this all seems really static and dull, by the way, then understand that you're getting a bona fide look at the reality of media life on the Trail, much of which consists of wandering around killing time on Bullshit 1 while you wait for the slight meaningful look from Travis that means he's gotten the word from his immediate superior, Todd (28 and so obviously a Harvard alum it wasn't ever worth asking), that after the next stop you're getting rotated up into the big leagues on the Express to sit squished and paralyzed on the crammed red press-couch in back and listen to John S. McCain and Mike Murphy answer the 'Twelve Monkeys' questions, and to look up-close and personal at McCain and the way he puts his legs way out on the salon's floor and crosses them at the ankle and sucks absently at his right bicuspid and swirls the coffee in his McCain2000.com mug, and to try to penetrate the innermost box of this man's thoughts on the enormous hope and enthusiasm he's generating in press and voters alike... which you should be told up front does not and cannot happen, this penetration, for two reasons. The smaller reason (1) is that when you are finally rotated up into the Straight Talk salon you discover that most of the questions the Twelve Monkeys ask back here are simply too vapid and obvious for McCain to waste time on, and he lets Mike Murphy handle them, and Murphy is so funny and dry and able to make such deliciously cruel sport of the 12M—

MONKEY: If, say, you win here in South Carolina, what do you do then?

MURPHY: Fly to Michigan that night.

MONKEY: And what if hypothetically you, say, *lose* here in South Carolina?

MURPHY: Fly to Michigan that night win or lose.

MONKEY: Can you perhaps explain why?

MURPHY: 'Cause the plane's already paid for.

MONKEY: I think he means: can you explain why specifically Michigan?

MURPHY: 'Cause it's the next primary.

MONKEY: I think what we're trying to get you to elaborate on if you will, Mike, is: what will your goal be in Michigan?

MURPHY: To get a whole lot of votes. That's part of our secret strategy for winning the nomination.

—that it's often hard even to notice McCain's there or what his face or feet are doing, because it takes almost all your concentration not to start giggling like a maniac at Murphy and at the way the 12M all nod somberly and take down whatever he says in their identical steno notebooks. The bigger and more interesting reason (2) is that this also happens to be the week in which John S. McCain's anticandidate status threatens to dissolve before almost everyone's eyes and he becomes increasingly opaque and paradoxical and in certain ways indistinguishable as an entity from the Shrub and the GOP Establishment against which he'd defined himself and shone so in New Hampshire, which of course is a whole story unto itself.

What's hazardous about Bullshit 1's lavatory door is that it opens and closes laterally, sliding with a *Star Trek*-ish whoosh at the light touch of the **DOOR** button just inside — i.e., you go in, lightly push **DOOR** to close, attend to business, lightly push **DOOR** again to open: simple — except that the **DOOR** button's placement puts it only inches away from the left shoulder of any male journalist standing over the commode attending to business, a commode without rails or handles or anything to (as it were) hold on to, and even the slightest leftward lurch or lean makes said shoulder touch said button — which keep in mind this is a moving bus — causing the door to whoosh open while you're right there with business under way, and with the consequences of suddenly whirling to try to stab at the button to reclose the door while you're *in medias res* being too obviously horrid to detail, with the result that by 9 February the great unspoken rule among the regulars on Bullshit 1 is that when a male gets up and goes two-thirds of the way back into the lavatory anybody who's back there clears the area and makes sure they're not in the door's line of sight; and the way you can tell that a journalist is local or newly rotated onto the Trail and this is his first time on BS1 is the small strangled scream you always hear when he's in the lavatory and the door unexpectedly whooshes open, and usually the grizzled old *Charleston Post and Courier* pencil will smile and call out "Welcome to national politics!" as the new guy stabs frantically at the button, and Jay at the wheel will toot the horn lightly with the heel of his hand in mirth, taking these long and mostly mindless DTs' fun where he finds it.

Coming back up Bullshit 1's starboard side, no laptops are in play and few window shades pulled, and the cleanest set of windows is just past the fridge, and outside surely the sun is someplace up there but the February vista still seems lightless. The central-SC countryside looks blasted, lynched, the skies the color of low-grade steel, the land all dead sod and broomsedge, with scrub oak and pine leaning at angles, and you can almost hear the mosquitoes breathing in their baggy eggs awaiting spring. Winter down here is both chilly and muggy, and Jay ends up alternating the heater with the AC as various different people bitch about being hot or cold. Scraggly cabbage palms start mixing with the pine as you get farther south, and the mix of conifer and palm is dissonant in a bad-dream sort of way. A certain percentage of the passing trees are dead and hung with kudzu and a particular type of Spanish moss that resembles a kind of drier-lint from hell. Eighteen-wheelers and weird tall pickups are the buses' only company, and the pickups are rusted and all have gun racks and right-wing bumper stickers; some of them toot their horns in support. BSI's windows are high enough that you can see right into the big rigs' cabs. The highway itself is colorless and the sides of it look chewed on, and there's litter, and the median strip is withered grass with a whole lot of different tire tracks and skidmarks striping the sod for dozens of miles, as if from the mother of all multivehicle pileups sometime in I-26's past. Everything looks dead and not happy about it. Birds fly in circles with no place to go. There are also some weird smooth-barked luminous trees that might be pecan; no one seems to know. The techs keep their shades pulled even though they have no laptops. You can tell it must be spooky down here in the summer, all wet moss and bog-steam and dogs with visible ribs and everybody sweating through their hat. None of the media ever seem to look out the window. Everyone's used to being in motion all the time. Location is mentioned only on phones: the journalists and producers are always on their cell phones trying to reach somebody else's cell phone and saying

"South Carolina! And where are you!" The other constant in most cell calls on a moving bus is "I'm losing you, can you hear me, should I call back!" A distinctive thing about the field producers is that they pull their cell phones' antennas all the way out with their teeth; journalists use their fingers, or else they have headset phones, which they talk on while they type.

Right now, in fact, most of the starboard side is people on cell phones. There are black cell phones and matte-gray cell phones; one MSNBC lady has a pink cell phone her fiancé got her from Hammacher Schlemmer. Some of the phones are so miniaturized that the mouthpiece barely clears the caller's earlobe and you wonder how they make themselves heard. There are headset cell phones of various makes and color schemes, some without antennas, plus the aforementioned earplug-and-hanging-podular-speaker cell phones. There are also pagers, beepers, vibrating beepers, voice-message pagers whose chips make all the voices sound distressed, and Palm Pilots that display CNN headlines and full-text messages from people's different 1-800 answering services, which all 27 of the media on BS1 have (1-800 answering services) and often kill time comparing the virtues of and relating funny anecdotes about. A lot of the cell phones have specially customized rings, which in a confined area with this many phones in play probably makes sense. There's one "Twinkle Twinkle Little Star," a "Hail Hail the Gang's All Here," one that plays the opening to Beethoven's Symphony No. 5 op. 67 in a weird 3/4 up-tempo, and so on. The only fly in the ointment here is that a *US News and W. R.* photographer, a Copley News Service pencil, and a leggy CNN producer who always wears red hose and a scrunchie all have the same "William Tell Overture" ring, so there's always some confusion and three-way scrambling for phones when a "William Tell Overture" goes off in transit. The network techs' phones all have regular rings.

Jay, the official Bullshit 1 driver and one of only two regulars aboard without a cell phone (he uses Travis's big gray Nokia when he needs to call one of the other bus drivers, which happens a lot because as Jay will be the first to admit he's a little weak in some of your navigational-type areas), carries a small attaché case full of CDs, and on long DTs he listens to them on a Sony Discman with big padded studio-quality headphones (which actually might be illegal), but Jay refuses to speak on-record to *Rolling Stone* about what music he listens to. John S. McCain himself is said to favor 60s classics and to at least be able to abide Fatboy Slim, which seems broad-minded indeed. The only other person who listens to headphones is a 12M who's trying to learn conversational Cantonese and whenever he's off the Express sits way back on BS1's port side with his Cantonese-lesson tapes and repeats bursts of inscrutable screeching over and over at a volume his headphones prevent him from regulating very well, and this guy often has a whole large area to himself. Travis, now again awake and in cellular contact with Todd up ahead on the Express, is in his customary precarious position at the very edge of a seat occupied by a wild-haired and slightly mad older Brit from the *Economist* who likes to talk at great length about how absolutely enraptured the British reading public is with John McCain and the whole populist-Tory McCain phenomenon, and tends to bore the hell out of everyone, but is popular anyway because he's an extraordinarily talented cabbager of hot food at mealtime events, and shares. The *Miami Herald* pencil in the seat next to them is reorganizing his Palm Pilot's address-book function by hitting tiny keys with what looks like a small black swizzle stick. There's also an anecdote under way by a marvelously caustic and funny Lebanese lady from Australia (don't ask) who writes for the *Boston Globe,* and is drinking a vanilla Edensoy and telling Alison Mitchell and the ABC field producer w/ earplug-phone across the aisle about apparently checking in and going up to her assigned room at the North Augusta Radisson last night and finding it already occupied by a nude male — "Naked as a jaybob. In his altogether. Starkers" — with only a washcloth over his privates — "and not a large one either, I can tell you," referring (as Alison M. later said she construed) to the washcloth.

The only BS1 regulars not covered so far are at the starboard work-table that's just past the edge of the crowded couch and behind the gang of techs at the front. They are CNN correspondent Jonathan Karl and CNN field producer Jim McManus (both of whom look about eleven) and their sound tech, and they're doing something interesting enough to warrant standing awkwardly balanced to watch and ignoring the slightly mad *Economist* guy's irritated throat-clearings at having somebody's unlaundered bottom swaying in the aisle right next to his head. The CNN sound tech (Mark A., 29, from Atlanta, and after Jay the tallest person on the Trail, vertiginous to talk to, able to get a stick's boom mike directly over McCain's head from the back of even the thickest scrum) has brought out from a complexly padded case a Sony SX-Series Portable Digital Editor ($32,000 retail) and connected it to some headphones and to Jonathan Karl's Dell Latitudes laptop and cell phone, and the three of them are running the CNN videotape of this morning's South Carolina Criminal Justice Academy address, trying to find a certain place where Jonathan Karl's notes indicate that McCain said something like "Regardless of how Governor Bush and his surrogates have distorted my position on the death penalty…" A digital timer below the SX's thirteen-inch screen counts seconds and parts of seconds down to four decimal places and is mesmerizing to watch as they fast-forward and Mark A. listens to what must be unimaginable FF chipmunkspeak on his headphones, waiting to tell Karl to stop the tape when he comes to what McManus says are the speech's "fighting words," which CNN HQ wants fed to them immediately so they can juxtapose the bite with something vicious the Shrub apparently said about McCain this morning in Michigan and do a breaking story on what-all Negative stuff is being said in the campaign today.

There's a nice opportunity here for cynicism about the media's idea of "fighting words" as the CNN crew FFs through the speech, Jim McManus eating his fifth Krispy Kreme of the day and awaiting Mark A.'s signal, Jonathan Karl polishing his glasses on his tie, Mark A. leaning forward with his eyes closed in aural concentration; and just behind Mark's massive shoulder, at the rear edge of the front starboard couch, is NBC camera tech Jim C., who has a bad case of the Campaign Flu, pouring more blood-red tincture of elderberry into a bottle of water, his expression carefully stoic because the elderberry remedy's been provided by his wife, who happens to be the NBC crew's field producer and is right across the aisle on the port couch watching him closely to see that he drinks it, and it'll be fun to hear Jim C. crack wise about the elderberry later when she's not around. Cynical observation: The fact that John McCain in this morning's speech several times invoked a "moral poverty" in America, a "loss of shame" that he blamed on "the ceaseless assault of violence-driven entertainment that has lost its moral compass to greed" (McCain's metaphors tend to mix a bit when he gets excited), and made noises that sounded rather a lot like proposing possible federal regulation of all US entertainment, which would have dicey constitutional implications to say the least—this holds no immediate interest for CNN. Nor are they hunting for the hair-raising place in the speech where McCain declared that our next president should be considered "Commander in Chief of the war on drugs" and granted the authority to send both money and (it sounded like) *troops,* if necessary, into "nations that seem to need assistance controlling their exports of poisons that threaten our children." When you consider that state control of the media is one of the big evils we point to to distinguish liberal democracies from repressive regimes, and that sending troops to "assist" in the internal affairs of sovereign nations has gotten the US into some of its worst messes of the last half century, these parts of McCain's speech seem like the real "fighting words" that a mature democratic electorate might care to hear the news talk about. But we don't care, evidently, and so neither do the networks. In fact, it's possible to argue that a big reason why so many young Independents and Democrats are excited about McCain is that the campaign media focus so much attention on McCain's piss-and-vinegar candor and so little attention on the sometimes *extremely* scary right-wing stuff this candor drives him to say... but no matter, because what's really riveting here at BS1's starboard table right now is what happens to McCain's face on the Sony SX's screen as they fast-forward through the speech's dull specifics. McCain has white hair (premature, from Hoa Lo), and dark eyebrows, and a pink scalp under something that isn't quite a comb-over, and kind of chubby cheeks, and in a regular analog fast-forward you'd expect his face to look silly, the way everybody on film looks spastic and silly when they're FF'd. But CNN's tape and editing equipment are digital, so what happens on FF is that the shoulders-up view of McCain against eight of the big flag's stripes doesn't speed up and get silly but rather just kind of *explodes* into myriad little digital boxes and squares, and these pieces jumble wildly around and bulge and recede and collapse and whirl and rearrange themselves at a furious FF pace, and the resultant image is like something out of the very worst drug experience of all time, a physiognomic Rubik's Cube's constituent squares and boxes flying around and changing shape and sometimes seeming right on the verge of becoming a human face but never quite resolving into a face, on the high-speed screen.

Who Even Cares
Who Cares

It's hard to get good answers to why Young Voters are so uninterested in politics. This is probably because it's next to impossible to get someone to think hard about why he's not interested in something. The boredom itself preempts inquiry; the fact of the feeling's enough. Surely one reason, though, is that politics is not cool. Or say rather that cool, interesting, alive people do not seem to be the ones who are drawn to the political process. Think back to the sort of kids in high school who were into running for student office: dweeby, over-groomed, obsequious to authority, ambitious in a sad way. Eager to play the Game. The kind of kids other kids would want to beat up if it didn't seem so pointless and dull. And now consider some of 2000's adult versions of these very same kids: Al Gore, best described by CNN sound tech Mark A. as "amazingly lifelike"; Steve Forbes, with his wet forehead and loony giggle; G. W. Bush's patrician smirk and mangled cant; even Clinton himself, with his big red fake-friendly face and "I feel your pain." Men who aren't enough like human beings even to hate—what one feels when they loom into view is just an overwhelming lack of interest, the sort of deep disengagement that is often a defense against pain. Against sadness. In fact, the likeliest reason why so many of us care so little about politics is that modern politicians make us sad, hurt us deep down in ways that are hard even to name, much less talk about. It's way easier to roll your eyes and not give a shit. You probably don't want to hear about all this, even.

One reason a lot of the media on the Trail like John McCain is simply that he's a cool guy. Non-dweeby. In school, Clinton was in student government and band, whereas McCain was a varsity jock and a hell-raiser whose talents for partying and getting laid are still spoken of with awe by former classmates, a guy who graduated near the bottom of his class at Annapolis and got in trouble for flying jets too low and cutting power lines and crashing all the time and generally being cool. At 63, he's witty, and smart, and he'll make fun of himself and his wife and staff and other pols and the Trail, and he'll tease the press and give them shit in a way they don't ever mind because it's the sort of shit that makes you feel that here's this very cool, important guy who's noticing you and liking you enough to give you shit. Sometimes he'll wink at you for no reason. If all that doesn't sound like a big deal, you have to remember that these pro reporters have to spend a lot of time around politicians, and most politicians are painful to be around. As one national pencil told *Rolling Stone* and another nonpro, "If you saw more of how the other candidates conduct themselves, you'd be way more impressed with [McCain]. It's that he acts somewhat in the ball-park of the way a real human being would act." And the grateful press on the Trail transmit—maybe even exaggerate—McCain's humanity to their huge audi-ence, the electorate, which electorate in turn seems so paroxysmically thankful for a presidential candidate *somewhat in the ballpark of a real human being* that it has to make you stop and think about how starved voters are for just some minimal level of genuineness in the men who want to "lead" and "inspire" them.

There are, of course, some groups of Young Voters who are way, way into modern politics. There's Rowdy Ralph Reed's far-Right Christians for one, and then out at the other end of the spectrum there's ACT UP and the sensitive men and angry womyn of the PC Left. It is interesting, though, that what gives these small fringe blocs such disproportionate power is the simple failure of most mainstream Young Voters to get off their ass and vote. It's like we all learned in social studies back in junior high: If I vote and you don't, my vote counts double. And it's not just the fringes who benefit—the fact is that it is to some very powerful Establishments' advantage that most younger people hate politics and don't vote. This, too, deserves to be thought about, if you can stand it.

There's another thing John McCain always says. He makes sure he concludes every speech and THM with it, so the buses' press hear it about 100 times this week. He always pauses a second for effect and then says: "I'm going to tell you something. I may have said some things here today that maybe you don't agree with, and I might have said some things you hopefully do agree with. But I will always. Tell you. The truth." This is McCain's closer, his last big reverb on the six-string as it were. And the frenzied standing-O it always gets from his audience is something to see. But you have to wonder. Why do these crowds from Detroit to Charleston cheer so wildly at a simple promise not to lie?

Well, it's obvious why. When McCain says it, the people are cheering not for him so much as for how good it feels to believe him. They're cheering the loosening of a weird sort of knot in the electoral tummy. McCain's résumé and candor, in other words, promise not empathy with voters' pain but relief from it. Because we've been lied to and lied to, and it hurts to be lied to. It's ultimately just about that complicated: it hurts. We learn this at like age four—it's grownups' first explanation to us of why it's bad to lie ("How would *you* like it if...?"). And we keep learning for years, from hard experience, that getting lied to sucks—that it diminishes you, denies you respect for yourself, for the liar, for the world. Especially if the lies are chronic, systemic, if experience seems to teach that everything you're supposed to believe in's really just a game based on lies. Young Voters have been taught well and thoroughly. You may not personally remember Vietnam or Watergate, but it's a good bet you remember "No new taxes" and "Out of the loop" and "No direct knowledge of any impropriety at this time" and "Did not inhale" and "Did not have sex with that Ms. Lewinsky" and etc. etc. It's painful to believe that the would-be "public servants" you're forced to choose between are all phonies whose only real concern is their own care and feeding and who will lie so outrageously and with such a straight face that you know they've just got to believe you're an idiot. So who wouldn't yawn and turn away, trade apathy and cynicism for the hurt of getting treated with contempt? And who wouldn't fall all over themselves for a top politician who actually seemed to talk to you like you were a person, an intelligent adult worthy of respect? A politician who all of a sudden out of nowhere comes on TV as this total long-shot candidate and says that Washington is paralyzed, that everybody there's been bought off, and that the only way to really "return government to the people" as all the other candidates claim they want to do is to outlaw huge unreported political contributions from corporations and lobbies and PACs...all of which are obvious truths that everybody knows but no recent politician anywhere's had the stones to say. Who wouldn't cheer, hearing stuff like this, especially from a guy we know chose to sit in a dark box for four years instead of violate a Code?

Even in AD 2000, who among us is so cynical that he doesn't have some good old corny American hope way down deep in his heart, lying dormant like a spinster's ardor, not dead but just waiting for the right guy to give it to? That John S. McCain III opposed making Martin Luther King's birthday a holiday in Arizona, or that he thinks clear-cut logging is good for America, or that he feels our present gun laws are not clinically insane — this stuff counts for nothing with these Town Hall crowds, all on their feet, cheering their own ability to finally really fucking *cheer.*

And are these crowds all stupid, or naive, or all over 40? Look again. And if you still think Young Voters as a generation have lost the ability — or transcended the desire — to believe in a politician, take a good look at *Time* magazine's shots of the South Carolina rave, or at the wire photos of Young NH Voters on the night McCain won there.

But then look at the photos of McCain's own face that night. He's the only one not smiling. Why? Can you guess? It's because now he might possibly win. At the start, on PBS and C-SPAN, in his shitty little campaign van with just his wife and a couple aides, he was running about 3 percent in the polls. And it's easy (or at least comparatively easy) to tell the truth when there's nothing to lose. New Hampshire changed everything. The 7 Feb. issues of all three big newsmagazines have good shots of McCain's face right at the moment the NH results are being announced. It's worth looking hard at his eyes in these photos. Now there's something to lose, or to win. Now it gets complicated, the campaign and the chances and the strategy; and complication is dangerous, because the truth is rarely complicated. Complication usually has more to do with mixed motives, gray areas, compromise. On the news, the first ominous rumble of this new complication was McCain's bobbing and weaving around questions about South Carolina's Confederate flag. That was a couple days ago. Now everybody's watching. Don't think the Trail's press have nothing at stake in this. There are two big questions about McCain now, today, as everyone starts the two-week slog through SC. The easy question, the one all the pencils and heads spend their time on, is whether he'll win. The other— the one posed by those photos' eyes —is hard to even put into words.

Negativity

7 to 13 February is pitched to *Rolling Stone* as a real "down week" on the GOP Trail, an interval almost breathtaking in its political unsexiness. Last week was the NH shocker; next week is the mad dash to SC's 19 Feb. primary, which the Twelve Monkeys all believe could now make or break both McCain and the Shrub. This week is the trenches: flesh-pressing,

fund-raising, traveling, poll-taking, strategizing, grinding out eight-event days in Michigan and Georgia and New York and SC. The Daily Press Schedule goes from twelve-point type to ten-. Warren MI Town Hall Meeting in Ukrainian Cultural Center. Saginaw County GOP Lincoln Day Dinner. Editorial Meeting w/ *Detroit News*. Press Conference at Weird Meth Lab–Looking Internet Company in Flint. Red-Eye to North Savannah on Chartered 707 with Faint *PanAm* Still Stenciled on Tail. Spartanburg SC Town Hall Meeting. Charleston Closed-Circuit TV Reception for McCain Supporters in Three States. AARP Town Forum. North Augusta THM. Live Town Hall Forum at Clemson U with Chris Matthews of MSNBC's *Hardball*. Goose Creek THM. Press Conference in Greenville. Door-to-Door Campaigning with Congressmen Lindsey Graham and Mark Sanford and Senator Fred Thompson (R-TN) and About 300 Media in Florence SC. NASCAR Tour and Test-Drive at Darlington Raceway. National Guard Armory THM in Fort Mill. Six Hours Flying for Two-Hour Fund-Raiser with NYC Supporters. Congressman Lindsey Graham Hosts Weird BBQ for a Lot of Flinty-Eyed Men in Down Vests and Trucker's Hats in Seneca SC. Book Signing at Chapter 11 Books in Atlanta. Taping of *Tim Russert Show* for CNBC. Greer THM. Cyber-Fund-Raiser in Charleston. *Larry King Live* with Larry King Looking Even More Like a Giant Bug than Usual.

Press-Avail in Sumter. Walterboro THM. On and on. Breakfast a Krispy Kreme, lunch a sandwich in Saran and store-brand chips, supper anyone's guess. Everyone but McCain is grim and tired. "We're in maybe a little bit of a trough in terms of excitement," Travis concedes in his orientation for new pencils on Monday morning...

...Until that very day's big tactical shift, which catches the McCain press corps unawares and gets all sorts of stuff under way for midweek's dramatic tactical climax, the Chris Duren Incident, all of which is politically sexy and exciting as hell, though not quite in the kind of way you cheer for.

The big tactical shift starts in the F&F Room of something called the Riverfront Hotel in the almost unbelievably blighted and depressing Flint MI, where all the Express's and Pimpmobile's media are at 1500h on 7 February while McCain is huddled with the staff High Command in a suite upstairs. In the primary campaign there is no more definitive behind-the-scenes locale than an F&F Room, which is usually some hotel's little third-string banquet- or meeting room off the lobby that McCain2000 rents (at the media's expense, precisely prorated and tallied, just like each day's seat on the buses and plane and the continental breakfasts before Baggage Call and even the F&F Rooms' "catered lunches," which today are strange bright-red ham on Wonder Bread, Fritos, and coffee that tastes like hot water with a brown crayon in it, and the pencils all bitch about the McCain2000 food and wistfully recount rumors that the Bush2000 press lunches are supposedly hot and multi–food group and served on actual plates by unctuous men with white towels over their arm) so that those media with PM deadlines can finish their stories and file and feed. In Flint, the F&F Room is a 60' × 50' banquet room with fluorescent chandeliers and overpatterned carpet and eight long tables with fax machines, outlets and jacks, and folding chairs (padded) for the corps to sit in and open notebooks and set up laptops and Sony SX- and DVS-Series Digital Editors and have at it. By 1515h, each chair is filled by a producer or pencil trying to eat and type and talk on the phone all at once, and there's an enormous bespectacled kid of unknown origin and status going around with NoGlare™ Computer Screen Light Filters and Power Strip™ Anti-Surge Eight-Slot Adapters and offering technical support for people whose laptops or phones are screwing up, and Travis and Todd and the other Press Liaisons are handing out reams of daily press releases, and the whole F&F Room is up and running and alive with the quadruple-ding of Windows booting up, the honk and static of modem connections, the multiphase clicking of 40+ keyboards, the needly screech of fax gear saying hi to New York and Atlanta, and the murmur of people on headset phones doing the same. The Twelve Monkeys have their own long table and are seated there in some very precise hierarchical order known only to them, each positioned exactly the same with his ankles crossed under his chair and a steno notebook and towering bottle of Evian at his left hand.

Everyone seems very touchy about anybody looking over their shoulder to see what they're working on.

Those McCain2000 media without any sort of daily deadline—meaning the techs, a very young guy from one of those weeklies that people can pick up free at Detroit supermarkets, and (after having no luck wandering around the tables trying to look over people's shoulders) *Rolling Stone*—are at the back of the F&F Room on a sort of very long makeshift ottoman composed of coats and luggage and non-hard cases of electronic gear. Even the network techs, practically Zen masters at waiting around and killing time, are bored out of their minds at today's F&F, where after racing back and forth to get all their gear off the bus in this bad neighborhood and making a chaise of it (the gear) here in the back there's nothing to do but they also can't really go anywhere because their field producer might suddenly need help feeding tape. The way the techs handle deep boredom is to become extremely sluggish and torpid, so that lined up on the ottoman they look like an exhibit of lizards whose tank isn't hot enough. Nobody reads. Pulse rates are about 40. The ABC cameraman lets his eyes almost close and naps in an unrestful way. The CBS and CNN techs, who like cards, today are not even bothering to play cards but are instead recounting memorable card games they've been in in the past. When *Rolling Stone* rejoins the techs here in the back there's a brief and not unkind discussion of deadline-journalism's privations and tensions and why looking over reporters' shoulders when they're typing is a faux pas. There are a lot of undistributed Power Strip adapters lying around, and for a while the techs do a gentle snipe hunting–type put-on of the Detroit-free-weekly kid involving plugging in a whole lot of multi-outlet Power Strips and playing something they claim is called Death Cribbage, complete with rules and fake anecdotes about games of Death Cribbage in past F&F Rooms, until Jim C. finally explains that they're just kidding and says the kid (who's extremely nervous-seeming and eager to please) might as well put all the Power Strips back.

It's taken less than a day to learn that the network techs—most of whom, granted, look and dress like aging roadies but are nevertheless 100 percent pro when it comes time to scrum or film a THM—are exponentially better to hang out with and listen to than anybody else on the Trail. It's true that McCain's younger staff and Press Liaisons are all very cool and laid-back and funny, with a very likable sort of Ivy

League–frathouse camaraderie between them (their big thing this week is to come up to each other and pantomime karate-chopping the person's neck and yell "Hiiii-*ya!*" so loudly that it annoys the Twelve Monkeys), but their camaraderie is insular, sort of like a military unit that's been through combat together, and they're markedly cautious and reserved around pencils, and even off-record won't talk very much about themselves or the campaign, clearly warned by the High Command to avoid diverting attention from their candidate or letting something slip that could hurt him in the press.

Even the techs can be guarded if you come on too strong. Here at the Flint F&F, one of the sound guys recounts an unverified and almost incredible incident involving some older tech friends of his actually *smoking dope* in the lavatory of then-candidate Jimmy Carter's campaign plane in Feb. '76—"There was some real wild shit went on back then, a lot more, like, you know, relaxed than the Trail is now"—but when he's asked for these older friends' names and phone numbers (another serious faux pas, Jim C. explains later) the sound guy's face clouds and he refuses both the names and permission to put the narrative in the *RS* notebook under any attribution less general than "one of the sound guys," so the incident is mentioned here only as unverified, and for the rest of the week this particular sound guy clams up completely whenever he sees *Rolling Stone* anyplace around, which feels both sad and kind of flattering.

"OTS" is, as previously mentioned, Trailese for "Opportunity to Smoke," which with very few exceptions only the techs seem to do—and do a *lot*—and which is prohibited on the buses even if you promise to exhale very carefully out the window; and so just about the only good thing about F&Fs is that they're basically one long OTS, although even here you have to go all the way outside in the cold and look at Flint, and the techs are required to get permission from their producers and let them know exactly where they'll be. Outside the Riverfront's side door off the parking lot, where it's so cold and windy you have to smoke with mittens on (a practice *Rolling Stone* in no way recommends), Jim C. and his longtime friend and partner Frank C. detail various other Trail faux pas and expand with no small sympathy on the brutality of these campaign reporters' existence: living out of suitcases and trying to keep their clothes pressed; praying that that night's hotel has room service; subsisting on the Campaign Diet, which is basically sugar and caffeine (diabetes is apparently the Black Lung of political journalism). Plus constant deadlines, and the pencils' only friends on the Trail are also their competitors, whose articles they're always reading but trying to do it secretly so they don't look insecure. Four young men in jackets over sweatshirts with the hoods all the way up are circling the press's Pimpmobile bus and boosting each other up to try the windows, and the two veteran techs just roll their eyes and wave. The Pimpmobile's driver is nowhere in sight—no one knows where drivers go during F&Fs (though there are theories). Also not recommended is trying to smoke in a high wind while jumping up and down in place. Plus, the NBC techs say, it's not just campaigns: political media are always on the road in some type of box for weeks at a time, very alone, connected to loved ones only by cell phone and 1-800 answering service. *Rolling Stone* speculates that this is maybe why everybody in the McCain2000 press corps, from techs to 12M, sports a wedding band—it's important to feel like there's someone to come home to. (His wife's slightly obsessive micromanagement of his health aside, Jim C. credits her presence on the Trail with preserving his basic sanity, at which Frank C. drolly credits his own wife's absence from the Trail with preserving same.) Neither tech smokes filtereds. *Rolling Stone* mentions being in hotels every night, which before the faux pas shut him down as a source the unnamed sound guy had said was probably the McCain campaign media's number-one stressor. The Shrub apparently stays in five-star places with putting greens and spurting-nymph fountains and a speed-dial number for the house masseur. Not McCain2000, which favors Marriott, Courtyard by Marriott, Hampton Inn, Signature Inn, Radisson, Holiday Inn, Embassy Suites. *Rolling Stone,* who is in no way cut out to be a road journalist, invokes the soul-killing anonymity of chain hotels, the rooms' terrible transient sameness: the ubiquitous floral design of the bedspreads, the multiple low-watt lamps, the pallid artwork bolted to the wall, the schizoid whisper of ventilation, the sad shag carpet, the smell of alien cleansers, the Kleenex dispensed from the wall, the automated wake-up call, the lightproof curtains, the windows that do not open—ever. The same TV with the same cable with the same voice saying "Welcome to _____" on its menu channel's eight-second loop. The sense that everything in the room's been touched by a thousand hands before. The sounds of others' plumbing. *RS* asks whether it's any wonder that over half of all US suicides take place in chain hotels. Jim and Frank say they get the idea. Frank raises a ski glove in farewell as the young men at the bus finally give up and withdraw. *RS* references the chain hotel's central paradox: the form of hospitality with none of the feeling—cleanliness becomes sterility, the politeness of the staff a vague rebuke. The terrible oxymoron of "hotel *guest*." Hell could easily be a chain hotel. Is it any coincidence that McCain's POW prison was known as the Hanoi *Hil-*

ton? Jim shrugs; Frank says you get used to it, that it's better not to dwell. Network camera and sound techs earn incredible overtime for staying in the field with a campaign over long periods. Frank C. has been with McCain2000 w/o break since early January and won't rotate out until Easter; the money will finance three months off during which he'll engineer indie records and sleep till eleven and not think once of hotels or scrums or the weird way your kidneys hurt after jouncing all day on a bus.

Monday afternoon, the first and only F&F in Michigan, is also *Rolling Stone*'s introduction to the Cellular Waltz, one of the most striking natural formations of the Trail. There's a huge empty lobbylike space you have to pass through to get from the Riverfront's side doors back to the area where the F&F and bathrooms are. It takes a long time to traverse this space, a hundred yards of nothing but flagstone walls and plaques with the sad pretentious names of the Riverfront's banquet/conference rooms—the Oak Room, the Windsor Room—but on return from the OTS now out here are also half a dozen different members of the F&F Room's press, each 50 feet away from any of the others, for privacy, and all walking in idle counterclockwise circles with a cell phone to their ear. These little orbits are the Cellular Waltz, which is probably the digital equivalent of doodling or picking at yourself as you talk on a regular landline. There's something oddly lovely about the Waltz's different circles here, which are of various diameters and stride-lengths and rates of rotation but are all identically counterclockwise and telephonic. We three slow down a bit to watch; you couldn't not. From above—if there were a mezzanine, say—the Waltzes would look like the cogs of some strange diffuse machine. Frank C. says he can tell by their faces something's up. Jim C., who's got his elderberry in one hand and cough syrup in the other, says what's interesting is that media south of the equator do the exact same Cellular Waltz, but that down there the circles are reversed.

And it turns out Frank C. was right as usual, that the reason press were dashing out and Waltzing urgently in the lobby is that sometime during our OTS word had apparently started to spread in the F&F Room that Mr. Mike Murphy of the McCain2000 High Command was coming down to do a surprise impromptu -Avail regarding a fresh two-page press release (still slightly warm from the Xerox) which Travis and Todd are passing out even now, and of which the first page is reproduced here:

FOR IMMEDIATE RELEASE   CONTACT: XXXXXXXXXXX
February 7, 2000   XXXXXXXXXXX

Bush Campaign Caught Red-Handed With Negative Ads, Unethical "Push-Polling"

Outraged South Carolinians Unite Against False Advertising, Universally Condemned Negative Polling Practice, McCain Volunteer Army Waiting With Tape Recorders to Catch Bush in the Act

COLUMBIA, SC — Deceptive TV ads and negative "push polls" conducted by phone in South Carolina last night by a polling firm employed by Texas Governor George W. Bush's campaign prompted outrage from Palmetto State voters who received the calls. One of these citizens joined Congressmen Lindsey Graham, SC House Majority Leader Rick Quinn and State Representative Dan Tripp at a press conference in Columbia today calling on Governor Bush to honor his pledge to run a positive campaign.

One of the most glaring distortions in the Bush TV ad is his contention that his plan puts $2 trillion into saving Social Security when, in fact, that money is required by law to be dedicated to the retirement plan. The other is the ad's false contention that former Congressman Vin Webber, a prominent McCain supporter, praised the Bush plan.

"George Bush's claim that he somehow invented the Social Security surplus is as true as Al Gore's claim to have invented the Internet," said Quinn. "The Bush plan doesn't add a nickel to the Social Security trust fund. The bottom line is that John McCain's plan is right and George W. Bush's plan – and his TV ad – are both dead wrong."

Push polling is the practice, condemned by political professionals in both parties, of conducting a phony poll which actually attacks an opponent with false or misleading accusations.

One South Carolinian who received the calls took extensive notes of the questions asked. The poll, conducted by Voter Consumer Research (Bush pollster Jan Van Lohuizen's company which identified itself at the beginning of each call and provided a phone number to that firm) "pushed" call recipients with "facts" such as:

- Do you agree with the part of [McCain's] tax plan that increases *taxes?* on contributions to colleges, charities and churches by $20 million?

The McCain tax plan does not tax charitable contributions. Under current law, a wealthy taxpayer can buy a painting for $10,000, have a "friendly" appraiser estimate its value at $100,000 and claim a deduction for the higher value by donating it to a charitable institution. This practice unfairly shifts the tax burden to middle income taxpayers.

--MORE--

XXXXXXXXXXXXXXXXXXXXXX
XXXXXXXXXXXXXXXXXXXXXXXXXXXXXXXXXXXXXXXXXX
XXXXXXXXXXXXXXXXXXXXXXXXXXXXXXXXXXXXXXXXXXXXXXXX

Paid for by McCain 2000, Inc.

This document is unusual not only because McCain2000's press releases are normally studies in bland irrelevance—"McCAIN TO CONTINUE CAMPAIGNING IN MICHIGAN TODAY"; "McCAIN HAS TWO HELPINGS OF POTATO SALAD AT SOUTH

CAROLINA VFW PICNIC"—but because no less a personage than Mike Murphy has indeed now just come down to spin this abrupt change of tone in the campaign's rhetoric. Murphy, who is only 37 but seems older, is the McCain campaign's Senior Strategist, a professional political consultant who's already had eighteen winning Senate and gubernatorial campaigns and is as previously mentioned a constant and acerbic presence in McCain's press salon aboard the Express. He's a short, bottom-heavy man, pale in a sort of yeasty way, with baby-fine red hair on a large head and sleepy turtle eyes behind the same type of intentionally nerdy hornrims that a lot of musicians and college kids now wear. He has short thick limbs and blunt extremities and is always seen either slumped low in a chair or leaning on something. Oxymoron or no, what Mike Murphy looks like is a giant dwarf. Among political pros, he has the reputation of being (1) smart and funny as hell, and (2) a real attack-dog, working for clients like Oliver North, New Jersey's Christine Todd Whitman, and Michigan's own John Engler in campaigns that were absolute operas of nastiness, and known for turning out what the *NY Times* delicately calls "some of the most rough-edged commercials in the business." He's leaning back against the F&F Room's wall in that way where you have your hands behind your lower back and sort of bounce forward and back on the hands, wearing exactly what he'll wear all week—yellow twill trousers and brown Wallabies and an ancient and very cool-looking brown leather jacket—and surrounded in a 180-degree arc by the Twelve Monkeys, all of whom have steno notebooks or tiny professional tape recorders out and keep clearing their throats and pushing their glasses up with excitement.

Murphy says he's "just swung by" to provide the press corps with some context on the strident press release and to give the corps "advance notice" that the McCain campaign is also preparing a special "response ad" that will start airing in South Carolina tomorrow. Murphy uses the words "response" or "response ad" nine times in two minutes, and when one of the Twelve Monkeys interrupts to ask whether it'd be fair to characterize this new ad as Negative, Murphy gives him a styptic look and spells *"r-e-s-p-o-n-s-e"* out very slowly. What he's leaning and bouncing against is the part of the wall between the room's door and the little round table still piled with uneaten sandwiches (to which latter the hour has not been kind), and the Twelve Monkeys and some field producers and lesser pencils form a half scrum around him, with various press joining the back or peeling away to go out and phone these new developments in to HQ.

Mike Murphy tells the hemispheric scrum that the press release and new ad reflect the McCain2000 campaign's decision, after much agonizing, to respond to what he says is Governor G. W. Bush's welching on the two candidates' public handshake-agreement in January to run a bilaterally positive campaign. For the past five days, mostly in New York and SC, the Shrub has apparently been running ads that characterize McCain's policy proposals in what Murphy terms a "willfully distorting" way. Plus there's the push-polling (see press release *supra*), a practice that is regarded as the absolute bottom-feeder of sleazy campaign tactics (Rep. Lindsey Graham, introducing McCain at tomorrow's THMs, will describe push-polling to South Carolina audiences as "the crack cocaine of modern politics"). But the worst, the most obviously unacceptable, Murphy emphasizes, was the Shrub standing up at a podium in SC a couple days ago with a wild-eyed and apparently notorious "fringe veteran" who publicly accused John McCain of "'abandoning his fellow veterans'" after returning from Vietnam, which, Murphy says, without going into Senator McCain's well-documented personal bio and heroic legislative efforts on behalf of vets for nearly 20 years (Murphy's voice rises an octave here, and blotches of color appear high on his cheeks, and it's clear he's personally hurt and aggrieved, which means that either he maybe really personally likes and believes in John S. McCain III or else has the frightening ability to raise angry blotches on his cheeks at will, the way certain great actors can make themselves cry on cue), is just so clearly over the line of even minimal personal decency and honor that it pretty much necessitates some kind of response.

The Twelve Monkeys, who are old pros at this sort

of exchange, keep trying to steer Murphy away from what the Shrub's done and get him to give a quotable explanation of why McCain himself has decided to run this response ad, a transcript of which Travis and Todd are now distributing from a fresh copier box and which is, with various parties' indulgence, also now reproduced here —

VIDEO COPY

RADIO: TELEVISION: XX

DATE: February 06, 2000 TIME: :30

PRODUCERS: Stevens Reed Curcio & Company

CLIENT: McCain 2000   *Draft*

TITLE: "Desperate "

CODE:

VIDEO: AUDIO:

McCain: "I guess it was bound to happen.

Governor Bush's campaign is getting desperate with a negative ad about me.

The fact is, I will use the surplus money to fix Social Security, cut your taxes, and pay down the debt.

Governor Bush uses all the surplus for tax cuts, with not one new penny for Social Security or the debt.

His ad twists the truth like Clinton. We're all pretty tired of that.

As President, I'll be conservative, and always tell you the truth, no matter what.

© 2000 All Rights Reserved.
Stevens Reed Curcio & Company.

—of which ad-transcript the 12M point out that in particular the "twists the truth like Clinton" part seems Negative indeed, since in '00 comparing a Republican candidate to Bill Clinton is roughly equivalent to claiming that he worships Satan. But Mike Murphy—part of whose job as Senior Strategist is to act as a kind of diversionary lightning rod for any tactical criticism of McCain himself—says that he, Mike Murphy, was actually the driving force behind the ad's "strong response," that he "pushed real hard" for the ad and finally got "the campaign" to agree only after "a great deal of agonizing, because Senator McCain's been very clear with you guys about wanting a campaign we can all be proud of." One thing political reporters are really good at, though, is rephrasing a query ever so slightly so that they're able to keep asking the same basic question over and over when they don't get the answer they want, and after several minutes of this they finally get Murphy to bring his hands out and up in a kind of what-are-you-gonna-do and to say "Look, I'm not going to let them go around smearing my guy for five days without retaliating," which then leads to several more minutes of niggling semantic questions about the difference between "respond" and "retaliate," at the end of which Murphy, reaching slowly over and poking at one of the table's sandwiches with clinical interest, says "If Bush takes down his negative ads, we'll pull the response right away. Immediately. Quote me." Then turning to go. "That's all I swung by to tell you." The back of his leather jacket has a spot of what's either Wite-Out™ or bird guano on it. Murphy is hard not to like, though in a very different way from his candidate. Where McCain comes off almost brutally open and direct, Murphy's demeanor is sly and cagey in a twinkly-eyed way that makes you think he's making fun of his own slyness. He can also be direct, though. One of the scrum's oldest and most elite 12M calls out one last time that surely after all there aren't any guns to the candidates' heads in this race, that surely Mike (the Monkeys call him Mike) would have to admit that simply refusing to "quote, 'respond' " to Bush and thereby "staying on the high road" was something McCain could have done; and Murphy's *dernier cri,* over his shoulder, is "You guys want a pacifist, go support Bradley."

For the remainder of the at least half hour more before John McCain is finally ready to get back on the Express (N.B.: McCain is later revealed to have had a sore throat today, apparently sending his staff into paroxysms of terror that he was coming down with the same Campaign Flu that's been ravaging the press corps [Jim C.'s own Campaign Flu will turn into bronchitis and then probably slight pneumonia, and for three days in South Carolina the whole rest of Bullshit 1's regulars will rearrange themselves to give Jim a couch to himself to sleep on during long DTs, because he's really sick, and it isn't until Friday that there's enough free time for Jim even to go get antibiotics, and still all week he's up and filming every speech and scrum, and in *RS's* opinion he is incredibly brave and uncomplaining about the Campaign Flu, unlike the Twelve Monkeys, many of whom keep taking their temperatures and feeling their glands and whining into their cell phones to be rotated out, so that by midweek in SC there are really only nine Monkeys, then eight Monkeys, although the techs, out of respect for tradition, keep referring to them as the Twelve Monkeys], and it later emerges that the Flint F&F was so protracted because Mrs. McC. and Wendy and McCain2000 Political Director John Weaver had McCain up there gargling and breathing steam and pounding echinacea) to head over to Saginaw, the techs, while checking their equipment and gearing up for the scrum at the Riverfront's main doors, listen to *Rolling Stone's* summary of the press release and Murphy's comments, confirm that the Shrub has indeed gone Negative (they'd heard about all this long before the Twelve Monkeys et al. because the techs and field producers are in constant touch with their colleagues on the Shrub's buses, whereas the Monkeys' Bush2000 counterparts are as aloof and niggardly about sharing info as the 12M themselves), and kill the last of the time in the Flint F&F by quietly analyzing Bush₂'s Negativity and McCain's response from a tactical point of view.

Leaving aside their aforementioned coolness and esprit de corps, you should be apprised that *Rolling Stone's* one and only journalistic coup this week is his happening to bumble into hanging around with these camera and sound guys. This is because network news techs—who all have worked countless campaigns, and who have neither the raging egos of journalists nor the political self-interest of the McCain2000 staff to muddy their perspective—turn out to be more astute and sensible political analysts than anybody you'll read or see on TV, and their assessment of today's Negativity developments is so extraordinarily nuanced and sophisticated that only a small portion of it can be ripped off and summarized here.

Going Negative is risky. Polls have shown that most voters find Negativity big-time distasteful, and if a candidate is perceived as getting nasty, it usually costs him. So the techs all agree that the first big question is why Bush2000 started playing the Negativity card. One possible explanation is that the Shrub was so personally shocked and scared by McCain's win in New Hampshire that he's now lashing out like a spoiled child and trying to hurt McCain however he can. The techs reject this, though. Spoiled child or no, Governor Bush is a creature of his campaign advisors, and these advisors are the best that $70,000,000 and the full faith and credit of the GOP Establishment can buy, and they are not spoiled children but seasoned tactical pros, and if Bush2000 has gone Negative there must be solid political logic behind the move.

This logic turns out to be indeed solid, even inspired, and the NBC, CBS, and CNN techs flesh it out while the ABC cameraman puts several emergency sandwiches in his lens bag for tonight's flight south on a campaign plane whose provisioning is notoriously inconsistent. The Shrub's attack leaves McCain with two options. If he does not retaliate, some SC voters will credit McCain for keeping to the high road. But it could also come off as wimpy, and so compromise McCain's image as a tough, take-no-shit guy with the courage to face down the Washington kleptocracy. Not responding might also look like "appeasing aggression," which for a candidate whose background is military and who spends a lot of time talking about rebuilding the armed forces and being less of a candy-ass in foreign policy would not be good, especially in a state with a higher percentage of both vets and gun nuts than any other (which SC is). So McCain pretty much has to hit back, the techs agree. But this is extremely dangerous, for by retaliating—which of course (despite all Murphy's artful dodging) means going Negative himself—McCain runs the risk of looking like just another ambitious, win-at-any-cost politician, when of course so much time and effort and money have already gone into casting him as the exact opposite of that. Plus an even bigger reason McCain can't afford to let the Shrub "pull him down to his level" (this in the phrase of the CBS cameraman, a Louisianan who's quite a bit shorter than the average tech and so besides all his other equipment has to lug a little aluminum stepladder around to stand on with his camera during scrums, which decreases his mobility but is compensated for by what the other techs agree is an almost occult talent for always finding the perfect place to set up his ladder and film at just the right angle for what his HQ wants—Jim C. says the tiny southerner is "technically about as good as they come") is that if Bush then turns around and retaliates against the retaliation and so McCain then has to re-retaliate against Bush's retaliation, and so on and so forth, then the whole GOP race could quickly degenerate into just the sort of boring, depressing, cynical, charge-and-countercharge contest that turns voters off and keeps them away from the polls... especially Young Voters, cynicism-wise, *Rolling Stone* and the underage pencil from the free Detroit weekly thing venture to point out, both now scribbling just as furiously with the techs as the 12M were with Murphy. The techs say well OK maybe but that the really important tactical point here is that John S. McCain *cannot* afford to have voters get turned off, since his whole strategy is based on exciting the people and inspiring them and pulling more voters *in*, especially those who'd stopped voting because they'd gotten so disgusted and bored with all the Negativity and bullshit of politics. In other words, *RS* and the Detroit-free-weekly kid propose to the techs, it's maybe actually in the Shrub's own political self-interest to let the GOP race get ugly and Negative and have voters get so bored and cynical and disgusted with the whole thing that they don't even bother to vote. Well no shit Sherlock H., the ABC techs in essence respond, good old Frank C. then explaining more patiently that, yes, if there's a low voter turnout, then the majority of the people who get off their ass and *do* vote will be the Diehard Republicans, meaning the Christian Right and the party faithful, and these are the groups that vote as they're told, the ones controlled by the GOP Establishment, an Establishment that as already mentioned has got all its cash and credibility invested in the Shrub. CNN's Mark A. takes time out from doing special stretching exercises that increase blood-flow to his arms (sound techs are very arm-conscious, since positioning a boom mike correctly in a scrum requires holding ten-foot sticks and 4.7-pound boom mikes [that's 4.7 without the weasel] horizontally out by their fully extended arms for long periods [which try this with an industrial broom or extension pruner sometime if you think it's easy], with the added proviso that the heavy mike at the end can't wobble or dip into the cameras' shot or [God forbid, and there are horror stories] clunk the candidate on the top of the head) in order to insert that this also explains why the amazingly lifelike Al Gore, over in the Democratic race, has been so relentlessly Negative and depressing in his attacks on Bill Bradley. Since Gore, like the Shrub, has his party's Establishment behind him, with all its organization and money and the Diehards who'll fall into line and vote as they're told, it's in Big Al's (and his party's bosses') interest to draw as *few* voters as possible into the Democratic primaries, because the lower the overall turnout, the more the Establishment voters' ballots actually count. Which fact then in turn, the short but highly respected CBS cameraman says, helps explain why, even though our elected representatives are always wringing their hands and making concerned noises about low voter turnouts, nothing substantive ever gets done to make politics less ugly or depressing or to actually induce more people to vote: our elected representatives are incumbents, and low turnouts favor incumbents for the same reason soft money does.

Let's pause here one second for a quick *Rolling Stone* PSA. Assuming you are demographically a Young Voter, it is again worth a moment of your valuable time to consider the implications of the techs' last couple points. If you are bored and disgusted by politics and don't bother to vote, you are in effect voting for the entrenched Establishments of the two major parties, who please rest assured are not dumb, and who are keenly aware that it is in their interests to keep you disgusted and bored and cynical and to give you every possible psychological reason to stay at home doing one-hitters and watching MTV on primary day. By all means stay home if you want, but don't bullshit yourself that you're not voting. In reality, there is *no such thing as not voting:* you either vote by voting, or you vote by staying home and tacitly doubling the value of some Diehard's vote.

So anyway, by this time all the press in the Flint F&F Room are demodemizing and ejecting diskettes and packing up their stuff and getting ready to go cover John McCain's 1800h speech at the GOP Lincoln Day Dinner in Saginaw, where a Republican dressed as Uncle Sam will show up on eight-foot stilts and totter around the dim banquet hall through the whole thing and nearly crash into the network crews' riser several times and irritate the hell out of everyone, and where the Twelve Monkeys will bribe or bullshit the head-waiter into seating them at a no-show table and feeding them supper while all the rest of the press corps has to stand in the back of the hall and try to help the slightly mad *Economist* guy cabbage breadsticks when nobody's looking. Watching the techs gear up to go scrum around McCain as he boards the Straight Talk Express is a little like watching soldiers outfit themselves for combat: there are numerous multipart packs and cases to strap across backs and chests and to loop around waists and connect and lock down, and pieces of high-priced machinery to load with filters and tape and bulbs and reserve power cells and connect to each other with complex cords and co-ax cable, and weasels to wrap around high-filter boom mikes, and sticks to choose and carefully telescope out all the way till they look like the probosces of some monstrous insect and bob, slightly—the soundmen's sticks and mikes do—as the techs in the scrum keep pace with McCain and try to keep his head in the center of their shot and right underneath the long stick's mike in case he says something newsworthy. McCain has on a fresh blue pinstripe suit, and his complexion is hectic with CF fever or tactical adrenaline, and as he passes through the Riverfront lobby toward the scrum there's a faint backwash of quality aftershave, and from behind him you can see Cindy McCain using her exquisitely manicured hands to whisk invisible lint off his shoulders, and at moments like this it's difficult not to feel enthused and to really like this man and want to support him in just about any sort of feasible way you can think of.

Plus there's the single best part of every pre-scrum technical gear-up: watching the cameramen haul their heavy $40,000 rigs to their shoulders like rocket launchers and pull the safety strap tight under

their opposite arm and ram the clips home with prac-
ticed ease, their postures canted under the camera's
weight. It is Jim C.'s custom always to say *"Up, Simba"*
in a fake-deep bwana voice as he hefts the camera to
his right shoulder, and he and Frank C. like to do a
little pantomime of the way football players will bang
their helmets together to get pumped for a big game,
although obviously the techs do it carefully and make
sure their equipment doesn't touch or tangle cords.

But so the techs' assessment, then, is that Bush$_2$'s
going Negative is both tactically sound and politically
near-brilliant, and that it forces McCain's own strategists to walk a very tight wire indeed. What McCain
has to try to do is retaliate without losing the inspiring high-road image that won him New Hampshire.
This is why Mike Murphy took valuable huddle-with-
candidate time to come down to the F&F and spoon-
feed the Twelve Monkeys all this stuff about Bush's
attacks being so far over the line that McCain had no
choice but to "respond." Because the McCain2000 campaign has got to spin today's retaliation the same way
nations spin war—i.e., McCain has to make it appear
that he is not actually being aggressive himself but is
merely repelling aggression. It will require enormous
discipline and cunning for McCain2000 to pull this
off. And tomorrow's "response ad"—in the techs'
opinion, as the transcript's passed around—this ad
is not a promising start, discipline-and-cunning-wise,

especially the "twists the truth like Clinton" line that the 12M jumped on Murphy for. This line's too mean. McCain2000 could have chosen to put together a much softer and smarter ad patiently "correcting" certain "unfortunate errors" in Bush's ads and "respectfully requesting" that the push-polling cease (with everything in quotes here being Jim C.'s suggested terms) and striking just the right high-road tone. The actual ad's "twists like Clinton" does not sound highroad; it sounds angry, aggressive. And it will allow Bush to do a React and now say that it's *McCain* who's violated the handshake-agreement and broken the 11th Commandment (= "Thou Shalt Not Speak Ill of Another Republican," which Diehard GOPs take very seriously) and gone way over the line...which the techs say will of course be bullshit, but it might be effective bullshit, and it's McCain's aggressive ad that's giving the Shrub the opening to do it.

If it's a mistake, then why is McCain doing it? By this time the techs are on the bus, after the hotel-exit scrum but before the Saginaw-entrance scrum, and since it's only a ten-minute ride they have their cameras down and sticks retracted but all their gear still strapped on, which forces them to sit up uncomfortably straight and wince at bumps, and in the Pimpmobile's mirrored ceiling they look even more like sci-fi combat troops on their way to some alien beachhead. The techs' basic analysis of the motivation behind "twists the truth like Clinton" is that McCain is genuinely, personally pissed off at the Shrub, and that he has taken Mike Murphy's leash off and let Murphy do what he does best, which is gutter-fight. McCain, after all, is known to have a temper (though he's been extremely controlled in the campaign so far and never shown it in public), and Jim C. thinks that maybe the truly ingenious thing the Shrub's strategists did here was find a way to genuinely, personally piss McCain off and make him want to go Negative even though John Weaver and the rest of the staff High Command had to have warned him that he'd be playing right into Bush2000's hands. This analysis suddenly reminds *Rolling Stone* of the thing in *The Godfather* where Sonny Corleone's fatal flaw is his temper, which Barzini and Tattaglia exploit by getting Carlo to beat up Connie and make Sonny so insanely angry that he drives off to kill Carlo and gets assassinated in Barzini's ambush at that tollbooth on the Richmond Parkway. Jim C., sweating freely and trying not to cough with 40 pounds of gear on, says he supposes there are some similarities, and Randy van R. (the taciturn but cinephilic CNN cameraman) speculates that the Shrub's brain-trust may actually have based their whole strategy on Barzini's ingenious ploy in *The Godfather,* whereupon Frank C. observes that $Bush_2$'s analog to slapping Connie Corleone around was standing up with the wacko Vietnam vet who claimed that McCain abandoned his comrades, which at first looked kind of stupid and unnecessarily nasty of Bush but from another perspective might have been sheer genius if it made McCain so angry that his desire to retaliate outweighed his political judgment. Because, Frank C. warns, this retaliation, and Bush's response to it, and McCain's response to Bush's response—this will be all that the Twelve Monkeys and the rest of the pro corps are interested in, and if McCain lets things get too ugly he won't be able to get anybody to pay attention to anything else.

It would, of course, have been just interesting as hell for *Rolling Stone* to have gotten to watch the top-level meetings at which John McCain and John Weaver and Mike Murphy and the rest of the campaign's High Command hashed all this out and decided on the press release and response ad, but of course strategy sessions like these are journalistically impenetrable, if for no other reason than that it is the media who are the true object and audience for whatever strategy these sessions come up with, the critics who'll decide how well it all plays (with Murphy's special little "advance notice" spiel in the Flint F&F being the strategy's opening performance, as everyone in the room was aware but no one said aloud).

But it turns out to be enough just getting to hear the techs kill time by deconstructing today's big moves, because events of the next few days bear out their analysis pretty much 100 percent. On Tuesday morning, on the Radisson's TV in North Savannah SC, both *Today* and *GMA* lead with "The GOP campaign takes an ugly turn" and show the part of McCain's new ad where he says "twists the truth like Clinton"; and sure enough by midday the good old Shrub has put out a React where he accuses John S. McCain of violating the handshake-agreement and going Negative and says (the Shrub does) that he (the Shrub) is "personally offended and outraged" at being compared to Bill Clinton; and at six THMs and -Avails in a row all around South Carolina McCain carps about the push-polling and "Governor Bush's surrogates' attacking [him] and accusing [him] of abandoning America's veterans," each time sounding increasingly reedy and peevish and with a vein that nobody's noticed before appearing to bulge and throb in his left temple when he starts in on the veteran thing; and then at a Press-Avail in Hilton Head the Shrub avers that he knows less than nothing about any so-called push-polling and suggests that the whole thing might have been fabricated as a sleazy political ploy on McCain2000's part; and then on Wednesday AM on TV at the Embassy Suites in Charleston there's now an even *more* aggressive ad that Murphy's gotten McCain to let him run, which new ad accuses Bush of unilaterally violating the handshake-agreement and going Negative and then shows a nighttime shot of 1600 Pennsylvania Ave.'s famous facade with its palisade of blatantly ejaculatory fountains in the foreground and says *"Can America afford another politician in the White House that we can't trust?,"* about which nobody mentions the grammatical problems but Frank C. says that the shot of the White House is really going low with the knife, and that if McCain loses South Carolina it may very well be because of this ad; and sure enough by Wednesday night focus polls are showing that South Carolina voters are finding McCain's new ad Negative and depressing, polls that the Shrub then seizes on and crows about while meanwhile Bush2000's strategists, "in response" to McCain's "outrageous" equation of $Bush_2$ with W. J. Clinton, which "impugns [Bush's] character and deeply offends [him]," start running a new ad of their own that shows a clip of the handshake in New Hampshire and then some photo of McCain looking angry and vicious and says "John McCain shook hands and promised a clean campaign, then attacked Governor Bush with misleading ads," then apparently just for good measure tosses in a sound bite from 4 Feb.'s *NBC Nightly News* that says "McCain solicited money from organizations appearing before his Senate Committee...and pressured agencies on behalf of his contributors," about which Jim C. (who, recall, works for NBC News) says the original *NBC Nightly News* report was actually just about Bush supporters' *charges* that

McCain had done these things, and thus that the ad's bite is decontextualized in a really blatantly sleazy and misleading way, but of course by this time—Thursday, 10 Feb., 0745h, proceeding in convoy formation to the day's first THMs in Spartanburg and Greenville—it doesn't matter, because there've been so many deeply offended charges and countercharges that McCain's complaining about the deceptive NBC bite would just be one more countercharge, which Jim C. says is surely why Bush2000 felt they could distort the bite and get away with it, which verily they appear to have done, because SC polls have both McCain's support and the primary's projected voter turnout falling like rocks, and the techs are having to spend all their time helping their field producers find the "fighting words" in every speech's tape because that's all the networks want, and everyone on Bullshit 1 & 2 is starting to get severely dispirited and bored, and even the 12M's strides have lost a certain pigeon-toed spring...

...And then out of nowhere comes the dramatic tactical climax mentioned way above, which hits the media like a syringe of epinephrine and makes all five networks' news that night. It occurs at the Spartanburg THM, whose venue is a small steep theater in the Fine Arts Center of a little college nobody ever did find out the name of, and is so packed by the time the McCain2000 press corps gets there that even the aisles are full, so that everybody except the techs and their producers is out in the lobby, which is itself teeming with college kids who couldn't get a seat either and are standing around taking notes for something called Speech Com 210—McCain's visit's apparently some sort of class assignment—and rather delighting *Rolling Stone* by continually looking over the 12M's shoulders to see what they're writing. Next to the free-pastry-and-sign-up-for-McCain2000-volunteering table is a huge oak column or stanchion or something, to each of whose four sides has been attached somehow a 24-inch color monitor that's tapping CNN's video feed, which stays tight on McCain's face against the backdrop's huge flag (Where do they *get* these giant flags? What happens to them when there's no campaign? Where do they go? Where do you even store flags that size? Or is there maybe just one, which McCain2000's advance team has to take down afterward and hurtle with to the next THM to get it put up before McCain and the cameras arrive? Do Gore and the Shrub and all the other candidates each have their own giant flag?), and if you pick your path carefully you can orbit the column very quickly and see McCain delivering his 22.5 to all points of the compass at once. The lobby's front wall is glass, and in the gravel courtyard just outside is a breathtaking 20-part Cellular Waltz going on around two local news vans throbbing at idle and raising their 40-foot microwave transmitters, plus four well-dressed local male heads with hand mikes doing their stand-ups, each attached to his tech by a cord. Compared to Schieffer and Bloom and the network talent on the ST Express, the local male heads always seem almost alienly lurid: their makeup makes their skin orange and their lips violet, and their hair's all so gelled you can see the heads' surroundings reflected in it. The local vans' transmitters' dishes, rising like great ghastly flowers on their telescoping poles, all turn to face identically south, their pistils aimed at Southeast Regional Micro-wave Relay #434B near Greenville.

To be honest, all the national pencils would proba-bly be out here in the lobby even if the theater weren't full, because after a few days McCain's opening THM 22.5 becomes wrist-slittingly dull and repetitive. Journalists who've covered McCain since Christmas report that Murphy et al. have worked hard on him to become more "message-disciplined," which in politicalspeak means reducing everything as much as possible to brief, memory-friendly slogans and then punching those slogans over and over. The result is that the McCain corps' pencils have now heard every message-disciplined bit of the 22.5—from McCain's opening joke about getting mistaken for a grampa at his children's school, to "It doesn't take much talent to get shot down," to "the Iron Triangle of money, lob-byists, and legislation," to "Clinton's feckless photo-op foreign policy," to "As president, I won't need any on-the-job training," to "I'm going to beat Al Gore like a drum," plus two or three dozen other lines that sound like crosses between a nightclub act and a motivational seminar—so many times that they just can't stand it anymore; and while they have to be at the THMs in case anything big or Negative happens, they'll go anywhere and do just about anything to avoid having to listen to the 22.5 again, plus of course to the laughter and cheers and wild applause of a THM crowd that's hearing it all for the first time, which is basically why the pencils are all now out here in the lobby ogling coeds and arguing about which silent-movie diva's the poor local heads' eyeshadow most resembles.

In fairness to McCain, he's not an orator and doesn't pretend to be. His real métier is conversation, a back-and-forth. This is because he's bright in a fast, flexible way that most other candidates aren't. He also genuinely seems to find people and questions and arguments energizing—the latter maybe because of all his years debating in Congress—which is why he favors Town Hall Q&As and constant chats with press in his rolling salon. So, while the media marvel at his accessibility because they've been trained to equate it with vulnerability, they don't seem to realize they're playing totally to McCain's strength when they converse with him instead of listening to his speeches. In conversation he's smart and alive and human and seems actually to listen and respond directly to you instead of to some demographic abstraction you might represent. It's his speeches and 22.5s that are canned and stilted, and also sometimes scary and right-wingish, and when you listen closely to these it's as if some warm pleasant fog suddenly lifts and it strikes you that you're not at all sure it's John McCain you want choosing the head of the EPA or the at least two new justices who'll probably be coming onto the Supreme Court in the next term, and you start wondering all over again what makes the guy so attractive.

But then the doubts again dissolve when McCain starts taking questions at THMs, which by now is what's under way in Spartanburg. McCain always starts this part by telling the crowd that he invites "questions, comments, and the occasional insult from any US Marines who might be here today" (which, again, gets radically less funny with repetition [apparently the Navy and Marines tend not to like each other]). The questions always run the great vox-populi gamut, from Talmudically bearded guys asking about Chechnya and tort reform to high-school kids reading questions off printed sheets their hands shake as they hold, from moms worried about their babies' future SSI to ancient vets in Legion caps who call McCain "Lieutenant" and want to trade salutes, plus the obligatory walleyed fundamentalists trying to pin him down on whether Christ really called homosexuality an abomination (w/ McCain, to his credit, pointing out that they don't even have the right Testament), and arcane questions about index-fund regulation and postal privatization, and HMO horror stories, and Internet porn, and tobacco litigation, and people who believe the Second Amendment entitles them to own grenade launchers. The questions are random and unscreened, and the candidate fields them all, and he's never better or more human than in these exchanges, especially when the questioner is angry or wacko — McCain will say "I respectfully disagree" or "We have a difference of opinion" and then detail his objections in lucid English with a gentleness that's never condescending. For a man with a temper and a reputation for suffering fools ungladly, McCain is unbelievably patient and decent with people at THMs, especially when you consider that he's 63, sleep-deprived, in chronic pain, and under enormous pressure not to gaffe or get himself in trouble. He doesn't. No matter how stale and message-disciplined the 22.5 at the beginning, in the Town Hall Q&As you get an overwhelming sense that this is a decent, honorable man trying to tell the truth to people he really sees. You will not be alone in this impression.

Among the techs and non-simian pencils, the feeling is that McCain's single finest human moment of the campaign so far was at the Warren MI Town Hall Meeting on Monday, in the Q&A, when a middle-aged man in a sportcoat and beret, a man who

didn't look in any way unusual but turned out to
be insane—meaning literally, as in *DSM IV*–grade
schizophrenic—came to the mike and said that the
government of Michigan has a mind-control machine
and influences brainwaves and that not even wrap-
ping roll after roll of aluminum foil around your head
with only the tiniest pinpricks for eyes and breathing
stopped them from influencing brainwaves, and he
says he wants to know whether if McCain is president
he will use Michigan's mind-control machine to catch
the murderers and pardon the Congress and compen-
sate him personally for 60 long years of government
mind control, and can he get it in writing. The question is not funny; the room's silence is the mortified
kind. Think how easy it would have been for a candidate here to blanch or stumble, or to have hard-eyed
aides remove the man, or (worst) to make fun of the
guy in order to defuse everyone's horror and embar-
rassment and try to score humor points with the crowd,
at which most of the younger pencils would probably
have fainted dead away from cynical disgust because
the poor guy is still standing there at the mike and
looking earnestly up at McCain, awaiting an answer.
Which McCain, incredibly, *sees*—the man's humanity, the seriousness of these issues to him—and says
yes, he will, he'll promise to look into it, and yes he'll
put this promise in writing, although he "believe[s]
[they] have a difference of opinion about this mind-

control machine," and in sum he defuses the insane man and treats him respectfully without patronizing him or pretending to be schizophrenic too, and does it all so quickly and gracefully and with such basic decency that if it was some sort of act then McCain is the very devil himself. Which the techs, later, after the post-THM Press-Avail and scrum, degearing aboard the ghastly Pimpmobile, say McCain is not (the devil) and that they were, to a man, moved by the unfakable humanity of the exchange, and yet at the same time also impressed with McCain's professionalism in disarming the guy, and Jim C. urges *Rolling Stone* not to be so cynical as to reject out of hand the possibility that the two can coexist—human genuineness and political professionalism—because it's the great yin-and-yang paradox of the McCain2000 campaign, and is so much more interesting than the sort of robotic unhuman all-pro campaign he's used to that Jim says he almost doesn't mind the grind this time.

Maybe they really can coexist—humanity and politics, shrewdness and decency. But it gets complicated. In the Spartanburg Q&A, after two China questions and one on taxing Internet commerce, as most of the lobby's pencils are still at the glass making fun of the local heads, a totally demographically average 30-something middle-class soccer mom in rust-colored slacks and those round, overlarge glasses totally average 30-something soccer moms always wear gets picked and stands and somebody brings her the mike. It turns out her name is Donna Duren, of right here in Spartanburg SC, and she says she has a fourteen-year-old son named Chris, in whom Mr. and Mrs. Duren have been trying to inculcate family values and respect for authority and a noncynical idealism about America and its duly elected leaders. They want him to find heroes he can believe in, she says. Donna Duren's whole story takes a while, but nobody's bored, and even out here on the stanchion's monitors you can sense a change in the THM's theater's voltage, and the national pencils come away from the front's glass and start moving in and elbowing people aside (which they're really good at) to get close to the monitors' screens. Mrs. Duren says that Chris—clearly a sensitive kid—was "made very very upset" by the Lewinsky scandal and the R-rated revelations and the appalling behavior of Clinton and Starr and Tripp and pretty much everybody on all sides during the impeachment thing, and Chris had a lot of very upsetting and uncomfortable questions that Mr. and Mrs. D. struggled to answer, and that basically it was a really hard time but they got through it. And then last year, at more or less a trough in terms of idealism and respect for elected authority, she says, Chris had discovered John McCain and McCain2000.com, and got interested in the campaign, and the parents had apparently read him some G-rated parts of McCain's

Faith of My Fathers, and the upshot is that young Chris finally found a public hero he could believe in: John S. McCain III. It's impossible to know what McCain's face is doing during this story because the monitors are taking CNN's feed and Randy van R. of CNN is staying hard and steady on Donna Duren, who appears so iconically prototypical and so thoroughly exudes the special quiet dignity of an average American who knows she's average and just wants a decent, noncynical life for herself and her family that she can say things like "family values" and "hero" without anybody rolling their eyes. But then last night, Mrs. D. says, as they were all watching some wholesome nonviolent TV in the family room, the phone suddenly rang upstairs, and Chris went up and got it, and Mrs. D. says a little while later he came back down into the family room crying and just terribly upset and told them the phone call had been a man who started talking to him about the 2000 campaign and asked Chris if he knew that John McCain was a liar and a cheater and that anybody who'd vote for John McCain was either stupid or un-American or both. That caller had been a push-poller for Bush2000, Mrs. Duren says, knuckles on her mike-hand white and voice almost breaking, distraught in a totally average and moving parental way, and she says she just wanted Senator McCain to know about it, about what happened to Chris, and wants to know whether anything can be done to keep people like this from calling innocent young kids and plunging them into disillusionment and confusion about whether they're stupid for trying to have heroes they believe in.

At which point (0853h) two things happen out here in the Fine Arts Center lobby. The first is that the national pencils disperse in a radial pattern, each dialing his cell phone, and the network field producers all come barreling through the theater doors pulling their cell phone antennas out with their teeth, and everybody tries to find a little empty area to Waltz in while they call the gist of this riveting Negativity-related development in to networks and editors and try to raise their counterparts in the Bush2000 press corps to see if they can get a React from the Shrub on Mrs. Duren's story, at the end of which story the second thing happens, which is that CNN's Randy van R. finally pans to McCain and you can see McCain's facial expression, which is pained and pale and looks actually more distraught even than Mrs. Duren's face had looked. And what McCain does, after staring down at the floor for a few seconds, is...apologize. He doesn't lash out at Bush$_2$ or at push-polling or appear to try to capitalize politically in any way. He looks sad and compassionate and regretful and says that the only reason he got into this race in the first place was to try to help inspire young Americans to feel better about devoting themselves to something, and that a story like what Mrs. Duren took the trouble to come down here to the THM this morning and tell him is just about the worst thing he could hear, and that if it's OK with Mrs. D. he'd like to call her son — he asks his name again, and Randy van R. pans smoothly back to Donna Duren as she says "Chris" and then pans smoothly back to McCain — Chris and apologize personally on the phone and tell Chris that yes there are unfortunately some bad people out there and he's sorry Chris had to hear stuff like what he heard but that it's never a mistake to believe in something, that politics is still worthwhile as a process to get involved in, and he really does look upset, McCain does, and almost as what seems like an afterthought he says that maybe one thing Donna Duren and other concerned parents and citizens can do is call the Bush2000 campaign and tell them to stop this push polling, that Governor Bush is a good man with a family of his own and it's difficult to believe he'd ever endorse his campaign doing things like this if he knew about it, and that he (McCain) will be calling Governor Bush again personally for the umpteenth time to ask him to stop the Negativity, and McCain's eyes now actually look wet, as in teary, which maybe is just a trick of the TV lights but is nevertheless disturbing, the whole thing is disturbing, because McCain seems upset in a way that's a little too...well, almost *dramatic*. He takes a couple more THM questions, then stops abruptly and says he's sorry but he's just so upset about the Chris Duren Incident that he's having a hard time concentrating, and he asks the THM crowd's forgiveness, and thanks them, and forgets his message-discipline and doesn't finish with he'll always. Tell them. The truth, but they applaud like mad anyway, and the four-faced column's monitors' feed is cut as Randy and Jim C. et al. go shoulder-held to join the scrum as McCain starts to exit.

And now none of this is simple at all, especially McCain's almost exaggerated-seeming distress about Chris Duren, which really did seem a little much; and a large set of disturbing and possibly cynical interconnected thoughts and questions start whirling around in the old journalistic head. Like the fact that Donna Duren's story was a far, far more devastating indictment of the Shrub's campaign tactics than anything McCain himself could say, and is it possible that McCain, on the theater's stage, wasn't aware of this? Is it possible that he didn't see all the TV field producers shouldering their way through the aisles' crowds with their cell phones and know instantly that Mrs. Duren's story and his reaction were going to get big network play and make Bush2000 look bad? Is it possible that some part of McCain could realize that what happened to Chris Duren is very much to his own political advantage, and yet he's still such a decent, uncalculating guy that all he feels is horror and regret that a kid was disillusioned? Was it human compassion that made him apologize first instead of criticizing the Shrub, or is McCain maybe just shrewd enough to know that Mrs. D.'s story had already nailed Bush to the wall and that by apologizing and looking distraught McCain could help underscore the difference between his own human decency and Bush's uncaring Negativity? Is it possible that he really had tears in his eyes? Is it (ulp) possible that he somehow *made* himself get tears in his eyes because he knew what a decent, caring, non-Negative guy it would make him look like? And come to think of it hey, why would a push-poller even be interested in trying to push-poll someone who's too young to vote? Does Chris Duren maybe have a really deep-sounding phone voice or something? But wouldn't you think a push-poller'd ask somebody's age before launching into his routine? And how come nobody asked this question, not even the jaded 12M out in the lobby? What could they have been thinking?

Bullshit 1 is empty except for Jay, who's grabbing an OTC way back in the ERPP, and through the port windows you can see all the techs and heads and talent in a king-size scrum around Mrs. Donna Duren in the gravel courtyard, and there's the additional cynical thought that doubtless some enterprising network crew is even now pulling up in front of poor Chris Duren's junior high (which unfortunately tonight on

TV turns out to be exactly what happened). The bus idles empty for a long time — the post-event scrums and stand-ups last longer than the whole THM did — and then when the BS1 regulars finally do pile in they're all extremely busy trying to type and phone and file, and all the techs have to get their SX and DVS Digital Editors out (the CBS machine's being held steady on their cameraman's little stepladder in the aisle because all the tables and the ERPP are full) and help their producers find and time the clip of Mrs. Duren's story and McCain's response so they can feed it to HQ right away, and the Twelve Monkeys have as one body stormed the Straight Talk Express, which is just up ahead on I-85 and riding very low in the stern from all the weight in McCain's rear salon. The point is that none of the usual media pros are available for *Rolling Stone* to interface with about the Chris Duren Incident and maybe get help from in terms of trying to figure out what to be cynical about and what not to and which of the many disturbing questions the whole Incident provokes are paranoid or irrelevant versus which ones might be humanly and/or journalistically valid... such as was McCain really serious about calling Chris Duren? How could he have even gotten the Durens' phone number when Mrs. D. was scrummed solid the whole time he and his staff were leaving? Does he plan to just look in the phone book or something? And where were Mike Murphy and John Weaver through that whole thing, who can usually be seen Cell-Waltzing back in the shadows at every THM but today were nowhere in sight? And is Murphy maybe even now in the Express's salon in his red chair next to McCain, leaning in toward the candidate's ear and whispering very calmly and coolly about the political advantages of what just happened and about various tasteful but effective ways they can capitalize on it and use it to get out of the tight tactical box that Bush$_2$'s going Negative put them in in the first place? What's McCain's reaction if that's what Murphy's doing — like is he listening, or is he still too upset to listen, or is he somehow both? Is it possible that McCain — maybe not even consciously — played up his reaction to Mrs. Duren's story and framed his distress in order to give himself a plausible, good-looking excuse to get out of the Negative spiral that's been hurting him so badly in the polls that Jim and Frank say he may well lose South Carolina if things keep on this way? Is it too cynical even to consider such a thing?

At the following day's first Press-Avail, John S. McCain III issues a plausible, good-looking, highly emotional statement to the whole scrummed corps. This is on a warm pretty 11 Feb. morning outside the Embassy Suites (or possibly Hampton Inn) in Charleston, right after Baggage Call. McCain informs the press that the case of young Chris Duren has caused him such distress that after a great deal of late-night soul-searching he's now ordered his staff to cease all Negativity and to pull all the McCain2000 response ads in South Carolina regardless of whether the Shrub pulls his own Negative ads or not.

And of course, framed as it is by the distressed context of the Chris Duren Incident, McCain's decision now in no way makes him look wimpy or appeasing, but rather like a truly decent, honorable, high-road guy who doesn't want young people's political idealism fucked with in any way if he can help it. It's a stirring and high-impact statement, and a masterful -Avail, and everybody in the scrum seems impressed and in some cases deeply and personally moved, and nobody (including *Rolling Stone*) ventures to point out aloud that, however unfortunate the phone call was for the Durens, it turned out to be just fortunate as *hell* for John S. McCain and McCain2000 in terms of this week's tactical battle, that actually the whole thing couldn't have worked out better for McCain2000 if it had been...well, like *scripted,* if like say Mrs. Donna Duren had been a trained actress or even gifted partisan amateur who'd been somehow secretly approached and rehearsed and paid and planted in that crowd of over 300 random unscreened questioners where her raised hand in that sea of average voters' hands was seen and chosen and she got to tell a moving story that made all five networks last night and damaged Bush$_2$ badly and now has released McCain from this week's tactical box. Any way you look at it (and there's a nice long DT in which to think about it), yesterday's Incident and THM were an almost incredible stroke of political luck for McCain … or else maybe a stroke of something else, something that no one — not the Twelve Monkeys, not Alison Mitchell or the marvelously cynical Australian *Globe* lady or even the totally sharp and unsentimental Jim C. — ever once broaches or mentions out loud, which might be understandable, since maybe even considering whether it was even *possible* would be so painful that it'd make it impossible to go on, which is what the press and staff and Straight Talk caravan and McCain himself have to do all day, and the next, and the next — go on.

Suck It Up

Another paradox: It is all but impossible to talk about the really important stuff in politics without using terms that have become such awful clichés they make your eyes glaze over and are difficult to even hear. One such term is "leader," which all the big candidates use all the time — as in "providing leadership," "a proven leader," "a new leader for a new century," etc. — and have reduced to such a platitude that it's hard to try to think about what "leader" really means and whether indeed what today's Young Voters want is a leader. The weird thing is that the word "leader" itself is cliché and boring, but when you come across somebody who actually *is* a real leader, that person isn't boring at all; in fact he's the opposite of boring.

Obviously, a real leader isn't just somebody who has ideas you agree with, nor is it just somebody you happen to believe is a good guy. A real leader is somebody who, because of his own particular power and charisma and example, is able to inspire people, with "inspire" being used here in a serious and non-cliché way. A real leader can somehow get us to do certain things that deep down we think are good and want to be able to do but usually can't get ourselves to do on our own. It's a mysterious quality, hard to define, but we always know it when we see it, even as kids. You can probably remember seeing it in certain really great coaches, or teachers, or some extremely cool older kid you "looked up to" (interesting phrase) and wanted to be like. Some of us remember seeing the quality as kids in a minister or rabbi, or a scoutmaster, or a parent, or a friend's parent, or a boss in some summer job. And yes, all these are "authority figures," but it's a special kind of authority. If you've ever spent time in the military, you know how incredibly easy it is to tell which of your superiors are real leaders and which aren't, and how little rank has to do with it. A leader's true authority is a power you voluntarily give him, and you grant him this authority not in a resigned or resentful way but happily; it feels right. Deep down, you almost always like how a real leader makes you feel, how you find yourself working harder and pushing yourself and thinking in ways you wouldn't be able to if there weren't this person you respected and believed in and wanted to please.

In other words, a real leader is somebody who can help us overcome the limitations of our own individual laziness and selfishness and weakness and fear and get us to do better, harder things than we can get ourselves to do on our own. Lincoln was, by all available evidence, a real leader, and Churchill, and Gandhi, and King. Teddy and Franklin Roosevelt, and probably de Gaulle, and certainly Marshall, and maybe Eisenhower. (Although of course Hitler was a real leader too, a very potent one, so you have to watch out; all it is is a weird kind of personal power.)

Probably the last real leader we had as US president was JFK, 40 years ago. It's not that Kennedy was a better human being than the seven presidents we've had since: we know he lied about his WWII record, and had spooky Mob ties, and screwed around more in the White House than poor old Clinton could ever dream of. But JFK had that special leader-type magic, and when he said things like "Ask not what your country can do for you; ask what you can do for your country," nobody rolled their eyes or saw it as just a clever line. Instead, a lot of them felt inspired. And

the decade that followed, however fucked up it was in
other ways, saw millions of Young Voters devote themselves to social and political causes that had nothing
to do with getting a plum job or owning expensive
stuff or finding the best parties; and the 60s were, by
most accounts, a generally cleaner and happier time
than now.

It is worth considering why. It's worth thinking
hard about why, when John McCain says he wants to
be president in order to inspire a generation of young
Americans to devote themselves to causes greater
than their own self-interest (which means he's saying
he wants to be a real leader), a great many of those
young Americans will yawn or roll their eyes or make
some ironic joke instead of feeling inspired the way
they did with Kennedy. True, JFK's audience was in
some ways more innocent than we are: Vietnam hadn't
happened yet, or Watergate, or the S&L scandals, etc.
But there's also something else. The science of sales
and marketing was still in its drooling infancy in 1961
when Kennedy was saying "Ask not..." The young people he inspired had not been skillfully marketed to all
their lives. They knew nothing of spin. They were not
totally, terribly familiar with salesmen.

Now you have to pay close attention to something
that's going to seem obvious at first. There is a difference between a great leader and a great salesman. There are also similarities, of course. A great

salesman is usually charismatic and likable, and he can often get us to do things (buy things, agree to things) that we might not go for on our own, and to feel good about it. Plus a lot of salesmen are basically decent people with plenty about them to admire. But even a truly great salesman isn't a leader. This is because a salesman's ultimate, overriding motivation is self-interest—if you buy what he's selling, the salesman profits. So even though the salesman may have a very powerful, charismatic, admirable personality, and might even persuade you that buying is in *your* interests (and it really might be)—still, a little part of you always knows that what the salesman's ultimately after is something for himself. And this awareness is painful...although admittedly it's a tiny pain, more like a twinge, and often unconscious. But if you're subjected to great salesmen and sales pitches and marketing concepts for long enough—like from your earliest Saturday-morning cartoons, let's say—it is only a matter of time before you start believing deep down that everything is sales and marketing, and that whenever somebody seems like they care about you or about some noble idea or cause, that person is a salesman and really ultimately doesn't give a shit about you or some cause but really just wants something for himself.

Some people believe that President Ronald W. Reagan (1981–89) was our last real leader. But not many of them are Young Voters. Even in the 80s, most younger Americans, who could smell a marketer a mile away, knew that what Reagan really was was a great salesman. What he was selling was the idea of himself as a leader. And if you're under, say, 35, this is what pretty much every US president you've grown up with has been: a very talented salesman, surrounded by smart, expensive political strategists and media consultants and spinmasters who manage his "campaign" (as in also "advertising campaign") and help him sell us on the idea that it's in our interests to vote for him. But the real interests that drove these guys were their own. They wanted, above all, To Be President, wanted the mind-bending power and prominence, the historical immortality—you could smell it on them. (Young Voters tend to have an especially good sense of smell for this sort of thing.) And this is why these guys weren't real leaders: because it was obvious that their deepest, most elemental motives were selfish, there was no chance of them ever inspiring us to transcend our own selfishness. Instead, they usually helped reinforce our market-conditioned belief that everybody's ultimately out for himself and that life is about selling and profit and that words and phrases like "service" and "justice" and "community" and "patriotism" and "duty" and "Give government back to the people" and "I feel your pain" and "Compassionate Conservatism" are just the politics industry's proven sales pitches, exactly the same way "Anti-Tartar" and "Fresher Breath" are the toothpaste industry's pitches. We may vote for them, the same way we may go buy toothpaste. But we're not inspired. They're not the real thing.

It's not just a matter of lying or not lying, either. Everyone knows that the best marketing uses the truth — i.e., sometimes a brand of toothpaste really *is* better. That's not the point. The point, leader-wise, is the difference between merely believing somebody and believing *in* him.

Granted, this is a bit simplistic. All politicians sell, always have. FDR and JFK and MLK and Gandhi were great salesmen. But that's not all they were. People could smell it. That weird little extra something. It had to do with "character" (which, yes, is also a cliché — suck it up).

All of this is why watching John McCain hold press conferences and -Avails and Town Hall Meetings (we're all at the North Charleston THM right now, 0820h on Wednesday, 9 Feb., in the horrible lobby of something called the Carolina Ice Palace) and be all conspicuously honest and open and informal and idealistic and no-bullshit and say "I run for president not to Be Somebody, but to Do Something" and "We're on a national crusade to give government back to the people" in front of these cheering crowds just seems so much more goddamn *complicated* than watching old b/w clips of John Kennedy's speeches.

It feels impossible, in February 2000, to tell whether John McCain is a real leader or merely a very talented political salesman, an entrepreneur who's seen a new market-niche and devised a way to fill it.

Because here's yet another paradox. Spring 2000—midmorning in America's hangover from the whole Lewinsky-and-impeachment thing—represents a moment of almost unprecedented cynicism and disgust with national politics, a moment when blunt, I-don't-give-a-shit-if-you-elect-me honesty becomes an incredibly attractive and salable and electable quality. A moment when an anticandidate can be a real candidate. But of course if he becomes a real candidate, is he still an anticandidate? Can you sell someone's refusal to be for sale?

There are many elements of the McCain2000 campaign—naming the bus "Straight Talk," the timely publication of *Faith of My Fathers,* the much-hyped "openness" and "spontaneity" of the Express's media salon, the message-disciplined way McCain thumps "Always. Tell you. The truth"—that indicate that some very shrewd, clever marketers are trying to market this candidate's rejection of shrewd, clever marketing. Is this bad? Or just confusing? Suppose, let's say, you've got a candidate who says polls are bullshit and totally refuses to tailor his campaign style to polls, and suppose then that new polls start showing that people really like this candidate's polls-are-bullshit stance and are thinking about voting for him because of it, and suppose the candidate reads these polls (who wouldn't?) and then starts saying even more loudly and often that polls are bullshit and that he won't use them to decide what to say, maybe turning "Polls are bullshit" into a campaign line and repeating it in every speech and even painting *Polls Are Bullshit* on the side of his bus.... Is he a hypocrite? Is it hypocritical that one of McCain's ads' lines in South Carolina is "Telling the truth even when it hurts him politically," which of course since it's an ad means that McCain is trying to get political benefit out of his indifference to political benefit? What's the difference between hypocrisy and paradox?

Unsimplistic enough for you now? The fact of the matter is that if you're a true-blue, market-savvy Young Voter, the only thing you're certain to feel about John McCain's campaign is a very modern and American type of ambivalence, a sort of interior war between your deep need to believe and your deep belief that the need to believe is bullshit, that there's nothing left anywhere but sales and salesmen. At the times your cynicism's winning, you'll find that it's possible to see even McCain's most attractive qualities as just marketing angles. His famous habit of bringing up his own closet's skeletons, for example — bad grades, messy divorce, indictment as one of the Keating Five — this could be real honesty and openness, or it could be

McCain's shrewd way of preempting criticism by criticizing himself before anyone else can do it. The modesty with which he talks about his heroism as a POW — "It doesn't take much talent to get shot down"; "I wasn't a hero, but I was fortunate enough to serve my time in the company of heroes" — this could be real humility, or it could be a clever way to make himself seem both heroic *and* humble.

You can run the same kind of either/or analysis on almost everything about this candidate. Even the incredible daily stamina he shows on the Trail — this could be a function of McCain's natural energy and enjoyment of people, or it could be gross ambition, a hunger for election so great that it drives him past sane human limits. The operative word here is "sane": the Shrub stays at luxury hotels like the Charleston Inn and travels with his own personal pillow and likes to sleep till nine, whereas McCain crashes at hellish chain places and drinks pop out of cans and moves like only methedrine can make a normal person move. Last night the Straight Talk caravan didn't get back to the Embassy Suites until 2340, and McCain was reportedly up with Murphy and Weaver planning ways to respond to Bush$_2$'s response to the Negative ad McCain's running in response to Bush$_2$'s new Negative ad for three hours after that, and you know getting up and showering and shaving and putting on a nice suit has to take some time if you're a guy who can't raise his arms past his shoulders, plus he had to eat breakfast, and the ST Express hauled out this morning at 0738h, and now here McCain is at 0822 almost running back and forth on the raised stage in a Carolina Ice Palace lobby so off-the-charts hideous that the press all pass up the free crullers. (The lobby's lined with red and blue rubber—yes, rubber—and 20 feet up a green iron spiral staircase is an open mezzanine with fencing of mustard-colored pipe from which hang long purple banners for the Lowcountry Youth Hockey Association, and you can hear the rink's organ someplace inside and a symphony of twitters and boings from an enormous video arcade just down the bright-orange hall, and on either side of the THM stage are giant monitors composed of nine identical screens arrayed 3 × 3, and the monitor on the left has nine identical McCain faces talking while the one on the right has just one big McCain face cut into nine separate squares, and every square foot of the nauseous lobby is occupied by wildly supportive South Carolinians, and it's at least 95 degrees, and the whole thing is so sensuously assaultive that all the media except Jim C. and the techs turn around and listen facing away, most drinking more than one cup of coffee at once.) And even on four hours' sleep at the very outside now McCain on the stage is undergoing the same metamorphosis that happens whenever the crowd is responsive and laughs at his jokes and puts down coffee and kids to applaud when he says he'll beat Al Gore like a drum. In person, McCain is not a sleek gorgeous telegenic presence like Rep. Mark Sanford or the Shrub. McCain is short and slight and stiff in a bit of a twisted way. He tends to look a little sunken in his suit. His voice is a thin tenor and not hypnotic or stirring per se. But onstage, taking questions and pacing like something caged, his body seems to dilate and his voice takes on a resonance, and unlike the Shrub he is bodyguardless and the stage wide open and the questions unscreened and he answers them well, and the best Town Meetings' crowds' eyes brighten, and unlike Gore's dead bird's eyes or the Shrub's smug glare McCain's own eyes are wide and candid and full of a very attractive inspiring light that's either devotion to causes beyond him or a demagogue's love of the crowd's love or an insatiable hunger to become the most powerful white male on earth. Or all three.

The point, to put it as simply as possible, is that there's a tension between what John McCain's appeal is and the way that appeal must be structured and packaged in order to get him elected. To get you to buy. And the media—which is, after all, the box in which John McCain is brought to you, and is for the most part your only access to him, and is itself composed of individual people, voters, some of them Young Voters—the media see this tension, feel it, especially the buses' McCain2000 corps. Don't think they don't. And don't forget they're human, or that the way they're going to resolve this tension and decide how to see McCain (and thus how to let you see McCain) will depend way less on political ideology than on each reporter's own little interior battles between cynicism and idealism and marketing and leadership. The far-Right *National Review*, for example, calls McCain "a crook and a showboat," while the old-Left *New York Review of Books* feels that "McCain isn't the anti-Clinton...McCain is more like the unClinton, in the way 7Up was the unCola: different flavor, same sugar content," and the politically indifferent *Vanity Fair* quotes Washington insiders of unknown affiliation saying "People should never underestimate [McCain's] shrewdness. His positions, in many instances, are very calculated in terms of media appeal."

Well no shit. Here in SC, the single most depressing and cynical episode of the whole week involves shrewd, calculated appeal. (At least in certain moods it looks like it does [maybe].) Please recall 10 February's Chris Duren Incident in Spartanburg and McCain's enormous distress and his promise to phone and apologize personally to the disillusioned kid. So the next afternoon, at a pre-F&F Press-Avail back in North Charleston, the new, unilaterally non-Negative McCain informs the press corps that he's going up to his hotel room right now to call Chris Duren. The phone call is to be "a private one between this young man and me," McCain says. Then Todd the Press Liaison steps in looking very stern and announces that only network techs will be allowed in the room, and that while they can film the whole call, only the first ten seconds of audio will be permitted. "Ten seconds, then we kill the sound," Todd says, looking hard at Frank C. and the other audio guys. "This is a private call, not a media event." Let's think about this. If it's a "private call," why let TV cameras film McCain making it? And why only ten seconds of sound? Why not either full sound or no sound at all?

The answer is modern and American and pretty much right out of Marketing 101. The campaign wants to publicize McCain's keeping his promise and calling a traumatized kid, but *also* wants to publicize the fact that McCain is calling him "privately" and not just exploiting Chris Duren for crass political purposes. There's no other possible reason for the ten-second audio cutoff, which cutoff will require networks that run the film to explain why there's no sound after the initial Hello, which explanation will then of course make McCain look doubly good, both caring and nonpolitical. Does the shrewd calculation of media appeal here mean that McCain doesn't really care about Chris Duren, doesn't really want to buck him up and restore the kid's faith in the political process? Not necessarily. But what it does mean is that McCain2000 wants to have it both ways, rather like big corporations that give to charity and then try to reap PR benefits by hyping their altruism in their ads. Does stuff like this mean that the gifts and phone call aren't "good"? The answer depends on how gray-area-tolerant you are about sincerity vs. marketing, or sincerity plus marketing, or leadership plus the packaging and selling of same.

But if you, like poor old *Rolling Stone,* have come to a point on the Trail where you've started fearing your own cynicism almost as much as you fear your own credulity and the salesmen who feed on it, you may find your thoughts returning again and again to a certain dark and box-sized cell in a certain Hilton half a world and three careers away, to the torture and fear and offer of release and a certain Young Voter named McCain's refusal to violate a Code. There were no techs' cameras in that box, no aides or consultants, no paradoxes or gray areas; nothing to sell. There was just one guy and whatever in his character sustained him. This is a huge deal. In your mind, that Hoa Lo box becomes sort of a special dressing room with a star on the door, the private place behind the stage where one imagines "the real John McCain" still lives. And but now the paradox here is that this box that makes McCain "real" is, by definition, locked. Impenetrable. Nobody gets in or out. This is huge, too; you should keep it in mind. It is why, however many behind-the-scenes pencils get put on the case, a "profile" of John

McCain is going to be just that: one side, exterior, split and diffracted by so many lenses there's way more than one man to see. Salesman or leader or neither or both, the final paradox — the really tiny central one, way down deep inside all the other campaign puzzles' spinning boxes and squares that layer McCain — is that whether he's truly "for real" now depends less on what is in his heart than on what might be in yours. Try to stay awake.